Creative Finishes

Creative
Finishes

Step-by-Step Techniques for Leafing, Sponging, Antiquing & More

Kass Wilson

Sterling Publishing Co., Inc.
New York

Prolific Impressions Production Staff:

Editor in Chief: Mickey Baskett
Copy Editor: Phyllis Mueller
Graphics: Karen Turpin
Styling: Lenos Key
Photography: Jerry Mucklow, Chris Little
Administration: Jim Baskett

Library of Congress Cataloging-in-Publication Data

Wilson, Kass.
  Creative finishes : step-by-step techniques for leafing, sponging, antiquing & more / Kass Wilson.
      p. cm.
  Includes index.
  ISBN-13: 978-1-4027-1467-2
  ISBN-10: 1-4027-1467-X
1. Texture painting. 2. Interior decoration. I. Title.
  TT323.W56 2006
  745.7'23--dc22

                                                   2005034549

2 4 6 8 10 9 7 5 3 1

Published by Sterling Publishing Co., Inc.
387 Park Avenue South, New York, NY 10016
© 2006 by Prolific Impressions, Inc.
Produced by Prolific Impressions, Inc.
160 South Candler St. Decatur, GA 30030
Distributed in Canada by Sterling Publishing
c/o Canadian Manda Group, 165 Dufferin Street,
Toronto, Ontario, Canada M6K 3H6
Distributed in the United Kingdom by GMC Distribution Services,
Castle Place, 166 High Street, Lewes, East Sussex, England BN7 1XU
Distributed in Australia by Capricorn Link (Australia) Pty. Ltd.
P.O. Box 704, Windsor, NSW 2756, Australia

Printed in China
All rights reserved

Sterling ISBN-13: 978-1-4027-1467-2
          ISBN-10: 1-4027-1467-X

For information about custom editions, special sales, premium and corporate purchases, please contact Sterling Special Sales Department at 800-805-5489 or specialsales@sterlingpub.com.

About the Artist

Kass Wilson has had a lifelong fascination with depth of color, dimension, and design that has motivated her journey into the world of finishes as a wall artisan. She has worked in the design industry for over 15 years, creating specialty finishes, murals, textures, and handmade papers.

Inspired by a passion for nature and a flair for the unconventional, she combines multiple mediums and techniques, creating innovative effects, both visual and tactile, on virtually any surface. Kass says, "Success for me is when you want to touch my art."

Her success is the result of years of dedicated study. Her work has been featured in numerous publications, show homes, and galleries. She has twice received awards from the Fauxcademy of Decorative Finishing.

Dedication

This book is dedicated to my sister, Elaine, who first encouraged me to follow my passion for creating beautiful environments. She forever believed in my talents more than I believed in myself. Her unending support has always been there for me through the difficult times. Now my wish is to share with her the joy of the fun times.

Contents

Proven Techniques for Professional Results

This book is intended to be as much an album of inspiration as it is a how-to guide. Its numerous photographs of actual interiors – not sets – dramatically reveal unlimited possibilities in the transformation from ordinary to extraordinary. The sections on specific procedures chronicle the attention to detail so necessary for developing finishes of depth and authenticity, showing you how and where you can create the unexpected.

My goal is to help you learn how to enhance a variety of surfaces. In this book, I share techniques I have used to produce nine types of creative finishes on walls, cabinetry, furniture, and decorative accessories. You'll also find numerous examples of color combinations for the various techniques and photographs that showcase my work in the homes of some of my clients.

Finishes you will learn to create:
    Striae Glaze Antiquing uses the bristles of a wall weaver brush or a china bristle brush to create fine lines of texture on a surface with tinted glaze, adding color and creating a mellow, aged look. When used with a wood-tone palette, striae glazing can simulate the look of wood.

    Crackling mimics the natural effects of time and weather on painted surfaces – when paint is applied over crackle medium, it forms separations and looks broken and shrunken. Glazing intensifies the crackling. You'll see how to create two types of crackling, random linear crackling and two-tone crackling (adding one or more colors that will show through the topcoat).

    The **Distressed Edging** technique shows how to use paint and glaze to create a rubbed, aged look without any sanding at all! Glazing softens the colors and imparts an aged look.

    Chamois and Brush Stippling are created by pouncing a tool on a glaze-coated surface. Tinted glaze adds color to a surface, providing a mottled look. For stippling, glaze is applied over a painted surface and the surface is pounced with a brush, removing some of the glaze to create a refined imprint of color and a gently aged look. Chamois tools can be used to produce textured effects with the look of top grain leather or the more organic look of stone.

Wood Graining gives the look of wood to surfaces by using glaze and a graining tool. It can be applied to doors, cabinets, trim, and furniture. It is an especially effective way to "refinish" a painted wooden door or to create the look of wood on furniture surfaces.

Stenciling is a traditional surface decorating technique where paint is applied through openings in a material that is resistant to paint to create a design. It can be used to create borders with repeating designs, corner and spot motifs, and words on walls.

Tissue Paper Texturing sandwiches crumpled tissue paper between two coats of paint to add dimensional texture to a surface. The surface is then washed with a glaze to heighten the texture. The technique can be used to cover entire walls or as a textural accent on accessories such as lampshades or candle holders. Varying the colors of tissue and paint offers endless possibilities.

Create the unexpected

The section on **Faux Metallic Leafing** explores two techniques – leafing a selected area and gold leafing applied in squares – that use metallic acrylic paint to mimic classic metal leafing techniques,

Highlighting adds a look of formal elegance to surfaces, enhancing raised details and adding interest and dimension to embellishments with a simple paint technique. An application of glaze tones and blends the metallic paint.

All the finishes in this book were created with waterbase (latex) products and simple tools that are readily available at paint stores, home improvement centers, and hardware stores. Unlike oil-based (alkyd) products, waterbase products are easy to clean up with soap and water. Their low volatile organic compound (VOC) composition creates very little odor and is safer for the environment.

With a little practice, you'll find it's easy to achieve professional results and create artful, interesting interiors. I hope you enjoy your journey.

About Paint

Choosing a quality paint is an important step in creating a
finish. The paint is the base of most finishes and determines the
color of the finished surface.

Latex Paints

I prefer latex paints for base painting surfaces because
of their easy cleanup, low odor, and quick drying time.
There are several good brands available at paint and hardware stores and home improvement centers. However,
not all paints are created equal – I find a great deal of dif-
ference from one brand to the next. Personal preference,
convenience, and the climate where you live are all fac-
tors in the equation. Following are the characteristics I
look for in a quality paint.

• **Degree of hardness.** Quality paint is hard and non-
porous when dry, allowing the glazes to slide or move
on the surface rather than soak in. Hardness also
affects the ultimate durability of the project.

   Because eggshell sheen paint has a harder, less
porous finish than flat paint, most of my finishes begin
with eggshell sheen basecoats or glossier.

• **Consistent, even coverage.** A good quality paint usually requires fewer coats for complete coverage. It may
cost more per gallon, but it ultimately costs less

because you'll need to apply fewer coats (and less of
your time is required).

• **Ability to level.** When applied to a surface, a good
quality paint will level out – that is, the paint evens out
on the surface and becomes flat, minimizing the
appearance of brush strokes or roller marks. A smooth
basecoat is essential for a good outcome.

• **UV protection.** UV protection inhibits paint from fading
or changing color when exposed to sunlight.

Acrylic Craft Paints

Acrylic paints that are found in the decorative painting
section of craft stores can be used to base paint small
projects. This paint is also used to mix with clear glazing
medium to create a transparent glaze for antiquing, stippling, and other techniques in this book. Acrylic craft
paints in pure artist pigment colors is the best type to use
to get the most intense and transparent mix. See more
about this in the "About Glazes" section. Stenciling is
also done with these types of paints.

*All the finishes in this book were created with waterbase products and simple
tools that are readily available at paint stores, home improvement centers, and
hardware stores. Unlike oil-based (alkyd) products, waterbase products are easy
to clean up with soap and water. Their low volatile organic compound (VOC)
composition creates very little odor and is safer for the environment.*

Glazes

Glazing is the basis for almost all the finishes in this book. A glaze is what is
applied over the base coat of paint to create the various finishes. It can be
manipulated with brushes, sponges, chamois or other tools to create
patterns and interesting textures. Glazes are very transparent and are tinted
with a colorant to create color that is darker than the base coat color.

Glazes, continued from page 10

Components of a Glaze

A glaze is made of two components, a **clear glazing medium** and a **colorant**. Glazing medium is clear paint that contains no pigment. It looks milky white in the container and, if applied to a surface, glazing medium would dry clear. Unlike some other paint products, glazing medium is slow drying, meaning it has a long working or open time. It gives you a longer window of opportunity to manipulate the product for the effect you want.

When glazing medium is tinted with a colorant, the resulting glaze is a sheer, transparent coating that imparts color and allows the underlying surface to show through. Much like looking through tinted cellophane, glazes produce layers or dimensions of color. Depending upon the ratio of paint to glaze, the working time may be reduced. (A higher concentration of paint equals less drying time.)

Various products can be used to color the clear glazing medium. **Pure artists' pigment colors** give the most translucence and dimension. Tinting with pre-mixed **acrylic paint** gives a more opaque look but is acceptable to use. You can also use a concentrated **color glaze** mixed into the clear glaze. Also available are **universal tints** that can be found at home centers. These work well to color glaze.

Mixing Glazes

The more colorant added to the glazing medium, the deeper and more intense the color. Exact recipes for glazes are difficult to devise – variables affecting the color of the glaze include everything from the thoroughness of the preparation and the type and color of the basecoat to the type of lighting in a room and the desired appearance. That is why it's ideal to mix the glaze on location, starting with a few drops of colorant and adding color until the result pleases you, so the intensity of the color can be judged in the conditions where it will be viewed every day.

Tips for Mixing Glazes

Make a sample board. Prepare a sample board with the same basecoat as your project surface. It should be large enough so you can test how long you have to work your wet edges. A sheet of posterboard works well for a sample board. Apply the tinted glaze to the sample using the same tool and technique that you plan to use for the project, and allow to dry. Just as paint tends to dry darker, so does glaze. Never depend on a wet sample to judge the end result. TIP: Use a hair dryer to speed up the drying time.

Start small. Start with small amounts of colorant – you can always add more. If you mix the glaze too strong, add more clear glazing medium. Never dilute glaze with water – it reduces the working time and makes the glaze more difficult to manipulate.

Mix enough. When mixing a glaze, begin with enough glazing medium to complete the project. You can calculate the amount of glaze you'll need by measuring the square footage you intend to cover and comparing that number with the coverage listed on the glazing medium container.

Record your recipe. Measure all ingredients as you mix and keep a record of the recipe. If you need to reproduce the color you'll know exactly how to do so.

Keep the leftovers. Store leftover glaze in an airtight plastic container (metal will rust). Label the container and keep it in a low-light, temperature-controlled place. Since each glaze is custom mixed, it will be priceless should you need to make a repair.

Handy Supplies & Equipment

These are the tools you need for just about every technique; other tools and supplies needed for specific techniques are listed in the techniques sections, where you'll also find more information about how to use these supplies.

- **Painter's tape**, for protecting walls, trim, and any areas you aren't trying to decorate. Painter's masking tape is blue and can be left in place for days (or longer – read the label inside the roll for the amount of time that can pass before it needs to be removed). When it's removed, there's no sticky residue.

- **Rags**, such as soft cotton rags like old t-shirts, cheesecloth, and old towels for rubbing out glazes. You can use rags or **paper towels** for a variety of tasks, including blotting, wiping, and cleaning up.

- **Buckets with lids**, for storing paints and glazes for the duration of your project.

- **Squeeze bottles** can be used for storing small amounts of glazes.

- **Mixers**, such as plastic forks for stirring in small containers and paint stirring sticks (get them when you buy paint) for mixing in buckets.

- **Drop cloths**, for protecting floors and furniture from paint spatters and drips

- **Sample boards**, for testing colors and finishes. They can be poster board, drywall, or wood. I always make a sample board, using the specific paints and glazes I've selected for the project, so I can test the intensity of the glaze colors in the light of the room where they will be applied.

- **Hair dryer**, for drying your samples. (Much faster than waiting for air drying!)

- **Disposable foam plates**, to use as palettes. I also use **paint trays** as palettes and to hold paint products when I use rollers to apply paints and glazes.

- **Straight edge**, for drawing straight lines.

- **Plastic containers with lids**, for storing leftover paints and glazes. Always label them clearly in case you need to do touchups later.

Surface Preparation

The outcome of your project depends greatly upon your surface preparation efforts, because each step in developing a creative finish builds on the previous layer. The effects of skipping steps may not be immediately apparent, but eventually they will show. That is why preparation can be considered the most important step.

Remove Hardware

When working on cabinets or furniture, remove hardware if possible. This will make your painting and finishing job much easier and neater.

Clean

The surface should be free of dirt, grease, and dust. Remove soil or grease from walls by washing with commercial cleaner meant to be used before painting, and follow the manufacturer's instructions for use.

Repair

A smooth, consistent surface is ideal. Make all repairs before you start to apply a creative finish. Fill any holes or dents with wood putty (on wood surfaces) or spackling compound (on drywall), and remove any flaking paint or splinters. Wearing a dust mask or respirator and working in adequate ventilation, sand the surface smooth. Remove sanding dust with a vacuum cleaner (for larger surfaces) or a tack cloth (for smaller pieces of furniture and accessories).

Prime

A good coat of primer seals a porous surface and creates a consistent surface that will bond with paint. Some primers also act as stain blockers. This is especially important over raw wood and previously damaged surfaces or when making a high contrast change in color. The type of primer to use depends on the type of surface you are painting. Ask your paint store professional to recommend an appropriate primer for your project.

Topcoats to Protect Your Finish

Clear sealers or varnishes provide additional durability and create a uniform sheen to the completed project. Using a sealer or varnish will keep your piece looking the same as when you finished it.

The specific product to use and the number of coats needed depends on the use a surface will receive. For example, the walls in a study usually will not experience as much wear and exposure to different elements (soil, grease, changes in temperature and humidity) as kitchen cabinets. For this reason, I usually apply three to four clear topcoats to cabinetry. Many walls require none.

When choosing a sheen for your topcoat or sealer, keep in mind that the higher the gloss, the more apparent surface imperfections may be. A higher gloss allows more light to reflect off the surface and draws attention to surface irregularities. As a result, brush strokes, roller marks, drips and less-than-perfect repairs will be more apparent with a glossier sheen.

Choose a topcoat that is non-yellowing and has excellent bonding properties with good chemical, water, and UV resistance. Consult your paint professional for recommendations.

Applying a Topcoat

Always start with a test sample of your completed finish. As you apply the topcoat, watch to make sure that the glaze is not reactivated and doesn't start to move. If it does, either the previous products have not fully cured or a sealer (barrier coat) may be needed.

Topcoats can be applied using a sprayer, a foam roller, or a high quality bristle brush. Applying a consistent topcoat requires patience and practice. Focus on even distribution of the product without overworking it.

Each layer of topcoat should be thin. Dilute the product according to the manufacturer's instructions. If applied too heavily, a hazy or milky appearance may result. In the event this occurs, wet sanding the surface in between coats may help.

Allow the surface to dry completely between coats. Keep in mind that the project may not completely cure for as long as 30 days.

Caring for Finished Surfaces

Treat your painted surfaces with care. Wipe with a damp soft cloth. **Never** scrub with abrasives or use ammonia or solvent-based products on a painted surface. ❑

Striae Glaze Antiquing

Striae glaze antiquing uses tinted glaze and the bristles of a wall weaver brush or a wallpaper brush to create fine lines of texture on a surface. This adds color to the surface and softens the colors of paint to create a mellow, aged look. When used with a wood-tone palette, striae glazing can simulate the look of wood.

Throughout this book, you'll see numerous examples of striae glaze antiquing on walls, cabinetry, and trim. In this section, you'll see photos that show you, step by step, how to create this finish on walls and on cabinet doors, plus examples of the technique in a variety of colors in kitchens and bathrooms.

Basic Supplies

Paints

Latex paint, eggshell sheen is needed for a basecoat on the wall or furniture piece.

Glaze

Clear glazing medium, to mix with a colorant to make an antiquing glaze

Colorant can be paint, a colored glaze or universal tint. It is mixed with the clear glazing medium to create the antiquing glaze.

Tools to Create Texture

Chip brushes or flat china bristle paint brushes in a variety of sizes, for applying glaze

Wall weaver brush, china bristle or stiff bristle brush, for creating the striae effect

Other Supplies

Laser level or bubble level, for creating a guide on walls

Plastic containers, for mixing the glaze (one for each glaze color)

A plastic fork, for mixing the glaze

Soft cloth rags, for wiping

Spray bottle with water, for dampening rags

Bristle brush and/or paint roller and tray, for applying the basecoat

Pictured clockwise from center top: Wall weaver brushes in two sizes, three sizes of china bristle or chip brushes, laser level.

Procedure for Walls

Prepare

1. Prepare the walls for painting, following the guidelines for cleaning, repairing, and priming in the section on *Surface Preparation*.
2. Tape off any molding or trim with painter's masking tape to protect them.
3. Use drop cloths to protect the floor or any furniture that's still in the room.
4. If you're planning to paint the ceiling, paint it before you paint the walls.

Basecoat

5. The basecoat or base paint is the first color applied to the surface and is the foundation of your creative finish. You can paint the basecoat with a brush, short-nap roller, or a paint sprayer. Apply as many coats as needed to achieve even, opaque coverage. Let dry between coats.

Mix the Glaze

6. Pour some glazing medium in a plastic tub or other container. Be sure to calculate enough for the entire project.
7. Add colorant to the container, a few drops at a time. **(photo 1)**
8. Mix to combine. **(photo 2)** I like to use a plastic fork. Continue to stir until the glaze color is completely mixed.

Apply Glaze to the Wall

9. Use a level to determine straight guidelines, especially when working on large areas. Taping plumb lines or using a laser level on a tripod can help as a guide. Avoid marking pencil lines as they could show through.
10. Use a wide chip brush to brush glaze on the wall, stroking in one direction from ceiling to floor or from top to bottom of a wall section. **(photo 3)** Attempt to pull the brush as straight as possible, following plumb lines. When working on walls, glaze only a small section of the wall at a time so you will be able to work the glaze before it dries – thin coats of glaze can dry quickly. But remember you must paint the small section from top to bottom.

Create the Striae Texture

12. Using a wallpaper brush or a wall weaver brush, pull the brush in a straight line down the entire length of the glazed section in one continuous motion. This will create tiny stripes of the glaze color. **(photo 6)** Concentrate on keeping the lines straight, and don't stop in the middle of the pull or the brush marks of the stopping and starting place will show. ❏

11. *Option:* If you want to use more than one glaze color, use a brush to apply it as you did the first color, overlapping the colors slightly **(photo 4)**, then apply more of the first color. **(photo 5)** Even when working with two colors, you will work in a small section, painting wall from top to bottom.

Striae Walls in Master Bath

Three glazes bring soft colors and texture to the white walls of this elegant bathroom retreat.

Supplies

Basecoat – Neutral White, a latex paint in eggshell sheen for painting walls

Glazes – Mushroom, Earth Green, Earth Brown. A glaze is the mixture of a glazing medium + colorant. You will need the colorant of your choice to produce glazes in these three colors. You can use acrylic pigments, acrylic paints, or universal tints in these colors or similar colors for tinting.

Chip brushes or flat paint brushes in a variety of sizes, for applying glaze

Wall weaver brush *or* wallpaper brush, for creating the striae effect

Laser level or bubble level, for determining guidelines on walls

Plastic containers, for mixing the glaze (one for each glaze color)

A plastic fork, for mixing the glaze

Soft cloth rags, for wiping

Spray bottle with water, for dampening rags

Bristle brush and/or paint roller and tray, for applying the basecoat

Sample board for testing results

Instructions

See the "Procedure for Walls" earlier in this section for details.

1. Prepare the walls for painting. Tape off the trim. Protect the floors and furniture.
2. Basecoat with Neutral White, applying as many coats as needed to achieve even, opaque coverage. Let dry between coats. Paint a sample board.
3. Mix the three colors of glazes using colorant plus the clear glazing medium. Try out the colors on the sample board.
4. Working one section at a time, apply the glazes to the wall, overlapping the colors slightly.
5. Brush to create the striae texture, pulling the brush in a straight line down the entire length of the glazed section in one continuous motion.
6. Repeat steps 4 and 5 to complete all the walls. ❏

Closeup of wall

Procedure for Cabinet Doors

Use this technique for applying striae glaze antiquing to dimensional surfaces such as trim, cabinet doors, mantles, or furniture.

Prepare

1. Remove hardware. Prepare the surface for painting, following the guidelines for cleaning, repairing, and priming in the section on Surface Preparation.
2. Tape off any walls or trim that you aren't planning to paint and glaze with painter's tape to protect them.
3. Use drop cloths to protect the floor or any adjacent surfaces.

Basecoat

4. Basecoat the surfaces with a brush, a short-nap roller, or a paint sprayer. Apply as many coats as needed to achieve even, opaque coverage. Let dry between coats.

Mix the Glaze

5. Pour some glazing medium in a plastic tub or other container. Add colorant to the container, a few drops at a time. Mix to combine. Be sure to mix enough for entire project.

Apply the Glaze

6. Apply the glaze to the cabinet casings first. Wipe off glaze. (See following section "Soften the Glaze with a Rag" for details.) Allow those areas to dry before proceeding to the doors.
7. Next, work on doors. Work glaze into corners of the cabinet trim by dabbing it into corners with a brush. **(photo 1)**
8. Apply glaze around the trim frame, following the direction of the stiles and rails. **(photo 2)**
9. Brush glaze around the outside of the frame, following the direction of the wood grain. **(photo 3)**

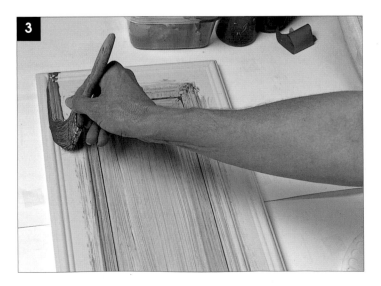

10. Work the glaze over the center panel, following grain direction. The door is now completely glazed. **(photo 4)**

You can stop here or proceed, depending on the look you want to achieve.

Soften the Glaze with a Rag

11. Working quickly so the glaze doesn't have a chance to dry, fold a soft flat rag to a workable size for your hand.
12. Use a spray bottle to dampen the rag with water. **(photo 5)**
13. Pull the damp rag across the high spots of the cabinet door to remove some of the glaze. **(photo 6)**
14. Continue wiping until you obtain the softness and contrast you desire. **(photo 7)**
    Note: You will need to work one section or one door at a time.

Protect Surface

15. Allow paint to thoroughly dry and cure. See manufacturer's recommendations.
16. Apply sealer or varnish to cabinets.
17. Replace hardware. ❏

Two-Tone Kitchen Cabinets

In this kitchen the same glaze color is used over two different basecoat colors. When separating colors horizontally, use the darker color below to add weight and ground the space. A thin band of the base cabinet color adorns the soffits. This is a clever way to pull the eye upward.
Décor designed by Peggy Daeger.

Before

Two-Tone Kitchen Cabinets

Supplies

Basecoat – Navajo White, a latex paint in eggshell sheen for painting upper cabinets

Basecoat – Rosemary Sprig, a latex paint in eggshell sheen for painting lower cabinets

Glaze – Earth Brown, clear glazing medium + colorant to create an Earth Brown glaze

Chip brushes or flat china bristle paint brushes in a variety of sizes, for applying glaze

Plastic containers, for mixing the glaze (one for each glaze color)

A plastic fork, for mixing the glaze

Soft cloth rags, for wiping

Spray bottle with water, for dampening rags

Bristle brush and/or paint roller and tray, for applying the basecoat

Sample board for testing results

Sealer or varnish of your choice for final protective topcoat

Instructions

See the "Procedure for Cabinet Doors" earlier in this section for details.

1. Prepare the cabinets for painting. Tape off trim and walls. Protect the floor and adjacent surfaces.
2. Basecoat the upper cabinets with Navajo White and the lower cabinets with Rosemary Sprig, applying as many coats as needed to achieve even, opaque coverage. Let dry between coats.
3. Mix the glaze.
4. Working the cabinet casings first, then one cabinet door at a time, brush the glaze on the surface in the direction of the wood grain.
5. Working quickly so the glaze doesn't have a chance to dry, use a damp rag to remove some of the glaze. Continue wiping until you obtain the softness and contrast you desire.
6. Repeat steps 4 and 5 to complete the cabinet. Remember to allow casings to dry before proceeding to doors.
7. Allow to dry. Apply sealer or varnish. Replace hardware. ❏

Closeup of cabinet

Green Kitchen Island

The painted center island adds interest and contrast to this large kitchen with wood-tone cabinets. The green tone was selected to enhance the colors of the granite counter.
Décor designed by Erin Stephenson

Supplies

Basecoat – Eucalyptus Leaf, a latex paint in eggshell sheen for painting island

Glaze – Deep Brown Espresso, clear glazing medium + colorant to create a Deep Brown Espresso glaze

Chip brushes or flat paint brushes in a variety of sizes, for applying glaze

Plastic containers, for mixing the glaze (one for each glaze color)

A plastic fork, for mixing the glaze

Soft cloth rags, for wiping

Spray bottle with water, for dampening rags

Bristle brush and/or paint roller and tray, for applying the basecoat

Sample board for testing results

Sealer or varnish of your choice for final protective coat

Instructions

See the "Procedure for Cabinet Doors" earlier in this section for details.

1. Prepare the island for painting. Tape off trim and walls. Protect the floor and adjacent areas.
2. Basecoat the island with Eucalyptus Leaf, applying as many coats as needed to achieve even, opaque coverage. Let dry between coats.
3. Mix the glaze.
4. Working on the cabinet casings first, then one door or drawer front of the island at a time, brush the glaze on the surface in the direction of the wood grain.
5. Working quickly so the glaze doesn't have a chance to dry, use a damp rag to remove some of the glaze. Continue wiping until you obtain the softness and contrast you desire.
6. Repeat steps 4 and 5 to complete the entire island. Allow casings to dry before proceeding to doors.
7. Allow to dry. Apply sealer or varnish. Replace hardware. ❑

Taupe & Black Kitchen Cabinets

One way to make a kitchen interesting, warm, and inviting is to incorporate different colors in different places with different finishes. This gives the impression that the space has been carefully furnished rather than factory produced and installed.

Here, a tone-on-tone finish applied to the cabinets and a black island with bronze metallic highlights create a rich impression.

Décor designed by Euna Williams

Before
The original all-white kitchen was cold and bland.

Taupe & Black Kitchen Cabinets

Taupe Cabinets & Trim

(See page 31 for closeups)

Supplies

Basecoat – Lenox Tan, a latex paint in eggshell sheen for painting cabinets

Glaze – Mushroom, for the larger, flatter surfaces

Glaze – Van Dyke Brown, for enhancing the grooves

Chip brushes or flat paint brushes in a variety of sizes, for applying glaze

Plastic containers, for mixing the glaze (one for each glaze color)

A plastic fork, for mixing the glaze

Soft cloth rags, for wiping

Spray bottle with water, for dampening rags

Bristle brush and/or paint roller and tray, for applying the basecoat

Sample board for testing results

Sealer or varnish for final protective coat

Instructions

See the "Procedure for Cabinet Doors" earlier in this section for details.

1. Prepare the cabinets for painting. Tape off trim, countertops, and walls. Protect the floor and adjacent surfaces.
2. Basecoat the cabinets with Lenox Tan, applying as many coats as needed to achieve even, opaque coverage. Let dry between coats.
3. Mix the two glaze colors.
4. Working on cabinet casings first, then one cabinet door, section of door, or drawer front at a time, brush the Mushroom glaze on the surface in the direction of the wood grain.
5. Working quickly so the glaze doesn't have a chance to dry, use a damp rag to remove some of the glaze. Continue wiping until you obtain the softness and contrast you desire.
6. Repeat steps 4 and 5 to complete the tan cabinets. Let dry.
7. Apply Van Dyke Brown glaze in the grooves and crevices.
8. Wipe off excess with a damp rag.
9. Allow to dry and cure. Apply sealer or varnish.
10. Replace hardware.

Black Cabinets

Supplies

Basecoat – Universal Black, a latex paint in eggshell sheen for painting cabinets

Glaze – Dark Brown, clear glazing medium + Dark Brown paint to produce a Brown glaze

Distressing Color – Metallic Bronze, for edges of cabinets

Foam brush for applying distressing color

Chip brushes or flat paint brushes in a variety of sizes, for applying glaze

Plastic containers, for mixing the glaze (one for each glaze color)

A plastic fork, for mixing the glaze

Soft cloth rags, for wiping

Spray bottle with water, for dampening rags

Bristle brush and/or paint roller and tray, for applying the basecoat

Sample board for testing results

Sealer or varnish for final protective coat

Instructions

The black cabinets were created with the Distressed Edging technique – see the "Distressed Edging" section for more details.

1. Remove the hardware. Prepare the cabinets for painting. Tape off trim and walls. Protect the floor and adjacent areas.

2. Basecoat with Universal Black, applying as many coats as needed to achieve even, opaque coverage. Let dry between coats.

3. Mix the glaze.

4. Working on cabinet casings first, then one cabinet door at a time, brush the glaze on the surface in the direction of the wood grain.

5. Working quickly so the glaze doesn't have a chance to dry, use a damp rag to remove some of the glaze. Continue wiping until you obtain the softness and contrast you desire. Remove most of the glaze from the distressed areas.

6. Repeat steps 4 and 5 to complete the cabinets. Complete casings and allow to dry before proceeding to doors.

7. Load the beveled edge of the foam brush with Metallic Bronze. Lightly stroke the raised parts of the door trim. Let dry.

8. Apply sealer or varnish.

9. Replace the hardware. ❏

Bathroom Cabinets

This easy striae technique gives these cabinets the look of wood graining because of the rich brown glaze colors used. The wood-tone finish is applied to all the cabinetry as well as the soffit. This draws the eye upward, acting to enhance the tall ceilings.

Décor designed by Erin Stephenson

Before

Bathroom Cabinets

Supplies

Basecoat – Greenfield Pumpkin, a latex in eggshell finish for painting cabinets

Glazes – Burnt Umber and Raw Umber, clear glazing medium + colorants to produce two colors of glazes – Burnt Umber and Raw Umber

Chip brushes or flat paint brushes in a variety of sizes, for applying glaze

Plastic containers, for mixing the glaze (one for each glaze color)

A plastic fork, for mixing the glaze

Soft cloth rags, for wiping

Spray bottle with water, for dampening rags

Bristle brush and/or paint roller and tray, for applying the basecoat

Sample board for testing results

Sealer or varnish for final protective coat

Instructions

See the "Procedure for Cabinet Doors" earlier in this section for details.

1. Prepare the cabinets, dressing table, tub base, and soffit for painting. Tape off trim, countertops, and walls. Protect the floor and adjacent surfaces.
2. Basecoat the cabinets, dressing table, tub base, and soffit with Greenfield Pumpkin, applying as many coats as needed to achieve even, opaque coverage. Let dry between coats.
3. Mix the glazes.
4. Working on the cabinet casings first, then one cabinet door, drawer front, or section at a time, brush Raw Umber glaze on the surface in the direction of the wood grain using a chip brush. Apply the Burnt Umber glaze in the grooves and crevices.
5. Working quickly so the glazes don't have a chance to dry, use a clean chip brush to pull across the glaze to create a soft grain. You want to make brush strokes so it gives the appearance of grain.
6. Repeat steps 4 and 5 to complete all the doors, drawer fronts, and panel surfaces.
7. On flat areas like the soffit, brush the glaze on the surface in the direction of the grain. Allow to dry
8. Stencil the design on the soffit with Burnt Umber glaze. See the section on Stenciling for Procedure Instructions.
9. Apply protective sealer or varnish. ❑

Before

Burgundy Kitchen Island

Specks of color in the granite counter were the inspiration for the base color of this kitchen island. The deep color is a pleasant contrast to the lighter wood floor and the overall light visual impression granite counter.

Supplies

Basecoat – Raisin Torte, a latex paint in eggshell sheen for painting the island

Glaze – Van Dyke Brown clear glazing medium + colorant to produce a Van Dyke Brown glaze

Chip brushes or flat paint brushes in a variety of sizes, for applying glaze

Plastic containers, for mixing the glaze (one for each glaze color)

A plastic fork, for mixing the glaze

Soft cloth rags, for wiping

Spray bottle with water, for dampening rags

Bristle brush and/or paint roller and tray, for applying the basecoat

Sample board for testing results

Sealer or varnish for protective final coat

Instructions

See the "Procedure for Cabinet Doors" earlier in this section for details.

1. Prepare the kitchen island for painting. Tape off trim, countertops, and walls. Protect the floor and adjacent surfaces.
2. Basecoat the island with Raisin Torte, applying as many coats as needed to achieve even, opaque coverage. Let dry between coats.
3. Mix the glaze.
4. Working on the cabinet casings first, then one cabinet door, drawer front, or section at a time, brush glaze on the surface in the direction of the wood grain and into the grooves and crevices.
5. Working quickly so the glaze doesn't have a chance to dry, use a damp rag to remove some of the glaze. Continue wiping until you obtain the softness and contrast you desire.
6. Repeat steps 4 and 5 to complete all the dimensional areas of the island.
7. Allow to dry. Apply sealer or varnish. Replace hardware. ❑

Closeup of cabinet

Colorways

Here are examples of color combinations. Do your own sample boards with your home décor colors for your own custom look.

Colorway 1
Basecoat – Black
Glaze – Metallic Eggplant

Colorway 2
Basecoat – White
Glaze – Payne's Gray

Colorway 3
Basecoat – Old Salem
  Gray
Glaze – Green Umber

Colorway 4
Basecoat – Sequoia
Glazes – Mahogany,
  Espresso

Crackling

Crackling techniques can give an aged distressed look to your furniture or cabinets. The usual causes of cracked paint are temperature, humidity, use/abuse, light exposure and dust. To achieve this look of authenticity, multiple techniques may be used on a single piece to represent different effects over time. True aging occurs randomly on a surface. As a result, I find it helpful while creating these projects to imagine how they may have been used or where they have been. For example, there would be more wear around handles, along edges or on tops. Dust settles on flat surfaces and in crevices. Sun shines inconsistently on vertical surfaces and causes layers of paint to split. By allowing your techniques to have random and subtle inconsistencies, the result will appear more hand and time crafted rather than factory produced.

The crackling process done with paint is a chemical reaction produced by the application of a crackle medium that alters the drying time of the paint layers. Paint that is applied over crackle medium forms cracks and looks broken and shrunken. By applying the crackle medium and the topcoat in the direction of the wood grain, a linear effect (crackles in the form of tiny lines) is achieved. This mimics the effects of time and weather on painted surfaces.

In this section, you'll see how to create two types of crackling, random crackling and two-color crackling (adding one or more colors that will show through the topcoat), plus numerous examples and colorways.

Basic Supplies

Paints

Latex paint, eggshell sheen, for the basecoat and topcoat. You may also need a second (and, sometimes, a third) paint color for two-tone crackling.

Glaze

Clear glazing medium, to mix with a colorant to make an antiquing glaze

Colorant can be paint, a colored glaze or universal tint. It is mixed with the clear glazing medium to create the antiquing glaze.

Tools & Other Supplies

Crackle medium, for creating the crackling. It's a clear liquid that is available in containers of various sizes, including small bottles and jars, quart cans, and tubs. Look for it at crafts, hardware, and paint stores and home improvement centers.

Chip brushes, for applying crackle medium, glazes and for spattering. Other options for spattering include an **old bristle brush or toothbrush**.

Plastic containers, for mixing the glaze (one for each glaze color)

A plastic fork, for mixing the glaze

Soft cloth rags, for wiping

Spray bottle with water, for dampening rags

Bristle brush and/or paint roller and tray, for applying the basecoat

Pictured above, top row: Three containers of crackle medium
Bottom row, left to right: Folded rag, chip brushes in three sizes

Random Linear Crackling

To achieve this look, crackle medium is applied to areas of a surface over a painted basecoat to create a random look of age and wear. When the crackle medium is dry, the same or another color topcoat is applied. The seemingly random cracks that form in the second coat of paint are intensified with glaze.

Prepare the Surface

1. Remove any hardware. Prepare the surface, following the guidelines for cleaning, repairing, and priming in the section on *Surface Preparation*.
2. Tape off any walls or trim that you aren't planning to paint and crackle with painter's tape to protect them.
3. Use drop cloths to protect the floor or any furniture that's still in the room.

Basecoat

NOTE: You can skip this step if your surface is already basecoated with an acrylic paint and you want that color to show through the cracks.

4. Basecoat the surfaces with a brush, short-nap roller, or a paint sprayer. Apply as many coats as needed to achieve even, opaque coverage. Let dry between coats.

Apply Crackle Medium

5. Choose the areas of the surface on which you would like cracks to appear. Brush crackle medium randomly over areas of the prepared surface. Use linear strokes in the direction you would like it to crack. **(photo 1)** The heavier the coat of crackle medium, the larger the cracks will appear. Brush on in a single stroke – do not brush back and forth or over work the medium. Allow medium to dry according to manufacturer's instructions.

Second Layer

6. Brush the basecoat color or a second color over the entire surface, including the areas with dried crackle medium, brushing in one direction only – **do not** over work or brush back and forth. **(photo 2)** Be sure to have an adequate coverage of paint for this coat. Cracks will begin to form within an hour. Let dry at least 24 hours to make sure crackling is complete.

Mix the Glaze

7. Pour some glazing medium in a plastic tub or other container.
8. Add colorant to the container, a few drops at a time. Mix to combine.

Apply the Glaze

9. Using a chip brush, brush glaze generously over the surface. The glaze will settle in the areas with crackled paint. **(photo 3)**

Wipe

10. Working quickly so the glaze doesn't have a chance to dry, fold a soft flat rag to a workable size for your hand. Use a spray bottle to dampen the towel with water.
11. Wipe off excess glaze with the cloth. **(photo 4)**
12. Continue wiping until you obtain the look you desire. Allow to dry.
13. Seal or varnish.
14. Replace the hardware. ❑

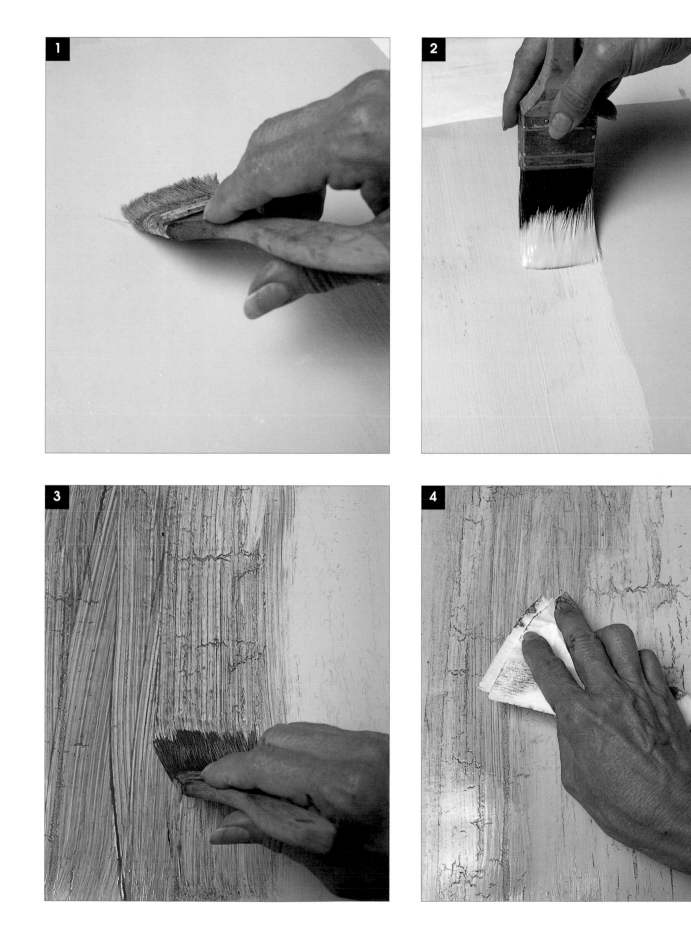

Bathroom Vanity

Bold and dramatic, the cabinetry becomes the focal point of the
bathroom. The original light color of the cabinetry shows through
the cracks, softened by glaze.
Décor designed by Connie Sharp

Supplies

Basecoat and Topcoat – Ruby Red, a latex paint in
eggshell sheen for painting cabinet

Glaze – Van Dyke Brown, clear glazing medium +
colorant to produce a dark brown glaze

Crackle medium, for creating the crackling. It's a clear
liquid that is available in containers of various sizes,
including small bottles and jars, quart cans, and tubs.
Look for it at crafts, hardware, and paint stores and
home improvement centers.

Chip brushes, for applying glazes and for spattering.
Other options for spattering include an **old bristle
brush or toothbrush.**

Plastic containers, for mixing the glaze (one for each
glaze color)

A plastic fork, for mixing the glaze

Soft cloth rags, for wiping

Spray bottle with water, for dampening rags

Bristle brush and/or paint roller and tray, for applying
the basecoat

Sample board for testing the results

Sealer or varnish for final protective coat

Instructions

*See the "Procedure for Random Crackling" earlier in this
section for details.*

1. Remove the hardware. Tape off trim, countertop, and
   walls. Protect the floor and fixtures.
2. Paint the surface of the cabinets.
3. Apply crackle medium to the areas of the surface on
   which you would like cracks to appear. Allow to dry.
4. Brush Ruby Red paint over the entire surface,
   including the areas with dried crackle medium,
   brushing in one direction only – **do not** brush back
   and forth. Cracks will form within an hour. Let dry.
5. Mix the glaze.
6. Working one section of the cabinet at a time, brush
   glaze on the surface in the direction of the wood grain
   and into the grooves and crevices. The glaze will settle in the areas with crackled paint.
7. Working quickly so the glaze doesn't have a chance to
   dry, use a damp rag to remove some of the glaze.
   Continue wiping until you obtain the softness and
   contrast you desire.
8. Repeat steps 6 and 7 to complete all the areas of the
   cabinet. Allow to dry.
9. Apply sealer or varnish.
10. Replace hardware. ❑

Yellow Mantle

A crackled and glazed painted finish establishes the mantle as the room's focal point and emphasizes its architectural details. *Décor designed by Diane Johnson*

Before

Yellow Mantle

Supplies

Basecoat – Yellow, a latex paint in eggshell sheen to paint the mantle (also used for edging)

Topcoat – Yellow, a latex paint in an eggshell sheen to paint over the crackle medium

Glaze – Espresso Brown, clear glazing medium + colorant to create a dark brown glaze

Crackle medium, for creating the crackling. It's a clear liquid that is available in containers of various sizes, including small bottles and jars, quart cans, and tubs. Look for it at crafts, hardware, and paint stores and home improvement centers.

Chip brushes, for applying glazes and for spattering. Other options for spattering include an **old bristle brush or toothbrush.**

Plastic containers, for mixing the glaze (one for each glaze color)

A plastic fork, for mixing the glaze

Soft cloth rags, for wiping

Spray bottle with water, for dampening rags

Bristle brush and/or paint roller and tray, for applying the basecoat

Sample board for testing the results

Sealer or varnish for final protective coat

Instructions

See the "Procedure for Random Crackling" earlier in this section for details.

1. Tape off trim and walls. Protect the floor and hearth.
2. Basecoat the mantle with Yellow.
3. Decide where you'd like the cracks to be and apply crackle medium to those areas. Allow to dry.
4. Brush a coat of Yellow paint over the entire surface, including the areas with dried crackle medium, brushing in one direction only – **do not** brush back and forth. Cracks will form within an hour. The heavier you apply the paint, the bigger the cracks will be. Let dry.
5. Use Coppertone to highlight the dimensional areas of the mantle and to edge some areas. See the sections on "Distressed Edging" and "Highlighting" for instructions.
6. Mix the glaze.
7. Working one section of the mantle at a time, brush glaze on the surface in the direction of the wood grain and into all the grooves and crevices. The glaze will settle in the grooves, crevices, and areas with crackled paint.
8. Working quickly so the glaze doesn't have a chance to dry, use a damp rag to remove some of the glaze. Continue wiping until you obtain the softness and contrast you desire.
9. Repeat steps 7 and 8 to complete all the areas of the mantle. Let dry.
10. Apply sealer or varnish. ❏

Yellow Hutch

This hutch is in a hallway between the kitchen and family room. Giving this hutch
a crackled, painted finish tied it into the adjacent kitchen as shown on page 54.
To create this finish, remove the hardware, follow the steps for the Yellow Mantle,
opposite, allow to dry, and replace the hardware.
The wallpaper was applied to the back of the center opening to match it to the
wallpaper on walls. Without the wallpaper, which visually anchors it to the rest of the
wall, the hutch would appear too heavy in scale for this space.
Décor designed by Diane Johnson

Before

Two-Color Linear Crackling

In this crackling technique, a basecoat is applied to the entire surface; then, in random areas, a second (and sometimes a third) paint color is applied here and there. Crackle medium is applied over the entire surface, rather than in just a few areas. When brushed with the basecoat color, the resulting cracks reveal the other paint color(s). An optional step shows how to "erase" some cracks. Rubbing with glaze gives an antique look that can be enhanced with optional spattering. You will need the same "Basic Supplies" as listed on page 41.

Prepare

1. Remove any hardware.
2. Prepare the surface, following the guidelines for cleaning, repairing, and priming in the section on Surface Preparation.
3. Tape off any walls or trim that you aren't planning to paint and crackle with painter's tape to protect them.
4. Use drop cloths to protect the floor or any adjacent surfaces.

Basecoat

5. Basecoat the surfaces with a brush, short-nap roller, or paint sprayer. Apply as many coats as needed to achieve even, opaque coverage. Let dry between coats.

Apply the Second Color

6. Randomly apply a second paint color to the basecoated surface in the areas where you want another color to show through the crackled area. **(photo 1)**

Apply Crackle Medium

7. Apply crackle medium over the entire surface, brushing in the direction of the wood grain and following the direction of the rails (vertical) and stiles (horizontal) on cabinet doors and drawers. Apply with a single stroke – do not brush back and forth. Let dry. **(photo 2)**

Topcoat with the Basecoat Color

8. Load a good quality bristle brush with the initial basecoat color – dip the brush into the paint and smooth out by brushing on a palette. The paint should be halfway up bristles of brush. **(photo 3)** (You want your brush well loaded because you are applying the color in one stroke, not brushing back and forth.)

9. Brush over the crackle medium with the loaded brush, following the wood grain and the direction of stiles and rails on the cabinet doors. **(photo 4)**
10. Let dry. As it dries cracks will form. The second paint color will show through the cracks. **(photo 5)** Allow to dry 24 hours for crackling to finish.

Option: Soften Cracks

11. To "erase" some of the crackling, paint over areas randomly with the basecoat color. **(photo 6)** This makes the crackling look more random and removes any areas that appear too harsh. Let dry.
12. To make the edges look worn, use the beveled edge of a foam brush to apply the second paint color to the edges of panels and raised areas – areas that would normally receive wear. **(photo 7)** The application should be random rather than uniform. Allow to dry.

Antique with Glaze

13. Begin by dabbing the glaze into the corners of trim **(photo 8)**.
14. Then brush glaze over the remainder of the area in the direction of the wood grain following stiles and rails. **(photo 9)**
15. *Option:* Wipe off some of the glaze with a soft, damp cloth. Allow to dry.

Spatter *Option:*

16. Mix glaze with water to thin it to an inky consistency.
17. Load a chip brush, a flat bristle brush, or an old toothbrush with the inky glaze.
18. Pull your finger across the bristles of the brush to spatter dots of glaze across the surface. **(photo 10)** TIP: To keep your hands clean, wear latex gloves.
19. Let dry thoroughly.
20. Apply sealer or varnish. Replace hardware. ❏

Red & Yellow Kitchen

The recipes for the finishes were developed to complement the wallpaper and accessories already in place. The deep red island stands out as a bold punch of color framed by vivid yellow cabinets. The deep brown background revealed by the crackling subtly brings the wood tones of the floor upward. The trim below the crown molding has been enhanced with color.

Décor designed by Diane Johnson

Before

Red & Yellow Kitchen

Yellow Cabinets

Supplies

Basecoat & Topcoat – Yellow, a latex paint in eggshell sheen

Second Color – Deep Brown, a latex paint in eggshell sheen

Glaze – Van Dyke Brown, a clear glazing medium + colorant mixed to produce a dark brown glaze

Crackle medium, for creating the crackling.

Chip brushes, for applying crackling medium, glazes and for spattering. Other options for spattering include an **old bristle brush or toothbrush**.

Plastic containers, for mixing the glaze (one for each glaze color)

A plastic fork, for mixing the glaze

Soft cloth rags, for wiping

Spray bottle with water, for dampening rags

Bristle brush and/or paint roller and tray, for applying the basecoat

Sample board for testing the results

Sealer or varnish for final protective coat

Instructions

See the "Procedure for Two-Color Crackling" earlier in this section for details.

1. Remove the hardware. Tape off trim and walls. Protect the floor and adjacent surfaces.
2. Basecoat the cabinets with Yellow.
3. Randomly apply areas of Deep Brown paint. Allow to dry.
4. Brush crackle medium over the surface. Let dry.
5. Brush a coat of Yellow paint over the entire surface, brushing in one direction only – **do not** brush back and forth – in the direction of the wood grain. Cracks will form with-

in an hour. The heavier you apply the paint, the bigger the cracks will be. Let dry 24 hours.
6. *Option:* "Erase" some of the crackling by re-painting areas randomly with the basecoat color. Let dry.
7. Mix the glaze.
8. Working one section of the cabinets at a time, brush glaze on the surface in the direction of the wood grain and into all the grooves and crevices. The glaze will settle in the grooves, crevices, and areas with

crackled paint.
9. Working quickly so the glaze doesn't have a chance to dry, use a damp rag to remove some of the glaze. Continue wiping until you obtain the softness and contrast you desire.
10. Repeat steps 8 and 9 to complete all the areas of the cabinets. Let dry.
11. *Option:* Spatter the cabinets with thinned glaze. Let dry.
12. Apply sealer or varnish. Replace the hardware. ❑

Red & Yellow Kitchen

Red Kitchen Island

This island is treated with the Striae Glaze Antiquing technique for a contrast to the yellow cabinets.

Supplies

Basecoat – Maple Leaf Red a latex paint in eggshell sheen to paint cabinets

Glaze – Van Dyke Brown, a clear glazing medium + colorant mixed to produce a dark brown glaze

Chip brushes or flat paint brushes in a variety of sizes, for applying glaze

China bristle brush, for creating the striae effect

Plastic containers, for mixing the glaze (one for each glaze color)

A plastic fork, for mixing the glaze

Soft cloth rags, for wiping

Spray bottle with water, for dampening rags

Bristle brush and/or paint roller and tray, for applying the basecoat

Sample board for testing results

Sealer or varnish for final protective coat

Before

Instructions

See the "Procedure for Striae Glaze Antiquing" for the steps to create this type of finish, using the colors listed above. ❏

Antiqued Gray Kitchen Cabinets

The colors in the wallpaper and countertops inspired this transformation. The homeowners had requested finishes that would never be found in a cabinetry showroom. Two paint colors, randomly applied, show through the crackling.

The island stands out because of its contrasting color and soft striae glazing. See the section on "Striae Glaze Antiquing" for instructions.

Before

Antiqued Gray Kitchen Cabinets

Supplies

Basecoat & Topcoat – Bennington Gray, a latex paint in an eggshell sheen to paint cabinets

Additional Colors – Leisure Green, Richmond Gold latex paints in an eggshell sheen

Glaze – Mushroom, clear glazing medium + color to create a dusty brown glaze

Crackle medium, for creating the crackling. It's a clear liquid that is available in containers of various sizes, including small bottles and jars, quart cans, and tubs. Look for it at crafts, hardware, and paint stores and home improvement centers.

Chip brushes, for applying glazes and for spattering. Other options for spattering include an **old bristle brush or toothbrush**.

Plastic containers, for mixing the glaze (one for each glaze color)

A plastic fork, for mixing the glaze

Soft cloth rags, for wiping

Spray bottle with water, for dampening rags

Bristle brush and/or paint roller and tray, for applying the basecoat

Sample board for testing the results

Sealer or varnish for final protective coat

Instructions

See the "Procedure for Two-Color Crackling" earlier in this section for details.

1. Remove the hardware. Tape off trim and walls. Protect the floor and adjacent surfaces.
2. Basecoat the cabinets with Bennington Gray. Make a sample board.
3. Randomly apply areas of Leisure Green and Richmond Gold paints. Allow to dry. Add some areas of both colors to the sample board.
4. Brush crackle medium over the surface. Let dry.
5. Brush a thick topcoat of Bennington Gray paint over the entire surface, brushing in one direction only – **do not** brush back and forth, in the direction of the wood grain. The heavier you apply the paint, the bigger the cracks will be. Let dry at least 24 hours.
6. *Option:* "Erase" some of the crackling by re-painting areas randomly with the basecoat color. Let dry.
7. Mix the glaze. Try out the color on the sample board.

Let dry.

8. Working one section of the cabinets at a time, brush glaze on the surface in the direction of the wood grain and into all the grooves and crevices. The glaze will settle in the grooves, crevices, and areas with crackled paint.
9. Working quickly so the glaze doesn't have a chance to dry, use a damp rag to remove some of the glaze. Continue wiping until you obtain the softness and contrast you desire.
10. Repeat steps 8 and 9 to complete all the areas of the cabinets. Let dry.
11. *Option:* Spatter the cabinets with thinned glaze. Let dry.
12. Apply sealer or varnish. Replace the hardware. ❑

Red Chest of Drawers

Using a buff color under the second coat of red paint gives the appearance that the
paint has worn away, revealing wood underneath. Striae glazing over the top
lends an additional rustic appearance.
Décor designed by Andrea Costa

Supplies

Basecoat & Topcoat – Mapleleaf Red, a latex paint in
eggshell sheen

Second Paint Color – Buff, a latex paint in eggshell
sheen

Glaze – Van Dyke Brown, clear glazing medium +
colorant mixed to produce a dark brown glaze

Crackle medium, for creating the crackling

Chip brushes, for applying glazes and for spattering.
Other options for spattering include an **old bristle
brush or toothbrush.**

Plastic containers, for mixing the glaze (one for each
glaze color)

A plastic fork, for mixing the glaze

Soft cloth rags, for wiping

Spray bottle with water, for dampening rags

Bristle brush and/or paint roller and tray, for applying
the basecoat

Sample board for testing the results

Sealer or varnish for final protective coat

Instructions

*See the "Procedure for Two-Color Crackling" earlier in
this section for details.*

1. Remove the hardware from the chest. Use a drop
   cloth to protect the floor and adjacent surfaces.
2. Basecoat the chest with Red.
3. Randomly apply areas of Buff paint. Allow to dry.
4. Brush crackle medium over the surface. Allow to dry
   according to manufacturer's instructions.
5. Brush a topcoat of Red paint over the entire surface
   in the direction of the wood grain, brushing in a
   single stroke, in one direction only – **do not** brush
   back and forth. The heavier you apply the paint, the
   bigger the cracks will be. Let dry.
6. *Option:* "Erase" some of the crackling by re-painting
   areas randomly with the basecoat color. Let dry.
7. Mix the glaze.
8. Working one section of the chest at a time, brush
   glaze on the surface in the direction of the wood grain
   and into all the grooves and crevices. The glaze will
   settle in the grooves, crevices, and areas with
   crackled paint.
9. Working quickly so the glaze doesn't have a chance to
   dry, use a damp rag to remove some of the glaze.
   Continue wiping until you obtain the softness and
   contrast you desire.
10. Repeat steps 8 and 9 to complete all the areas of the
    chest. Let dry.
11. Apply sealer or varnish. Replace the hardware. ❏

Closeup

Bar Stools

Décor designed by Andrea Costa

Supplies

Basecoat & Topcoat – Mapleleaf Red, a latex paint in eggshell sheen

Second Paint Color – Buff, a latex paint in eggshell sheen

Glaze – Van Dyke Brown, clear glazing medium + colorant mixed to produce a dark brown glaze

Crackle medium, for creating the crackling

Chip brushes, for applying glazes and for spattering. Other options for spattering include an **old bristle brush or toothbrush.**

Plastic containers, for mixing the glaze (one for each glaze color)

A plastic fork, for mixing the glaze

Soft cloth rags, for wiping

Spray bottle with water, for dampening rags

Bristle brush and/or paint roller and tray, for applying the basecoat

Sample board for testing the results

Sealer or varnish for final protective coat

Instructions

See the "Procedure for Two-Color Crackling" earlier in this section for details.

1. Prepare the surfaces for painting. Tape off areas you don't want to paint. Use a drop cloth to protect the floor.
2. Basecoat the bar stools with Red. Paint the sample board.
3. Randomly apply areas of Buff paint to the bar stools, using the project photo as a guide. Allow to dry. Add some areas of the paint to the sample board.
4. Brush crackle medium over the surfaces. Let dry according to manufacturer's instructions.
5. Brush a topcoat of Red paint over all the surfaces in the direction of the wood grain, brushing on in a single stroke – **do not** brush back and forth. The heavier you apply the paint, the bigger the cracks will be. Let dry. Paint the sample board.
6. *Option:* "Erase" some of the crackling by re-painting areas randomly with the red basecoat color. Let dry.
7. Mix the glaze. Try out the color on the sample board. Let dry.
8. Brush glaze on the surface in the direction of the wood grain and into all the grooves and crevices. The glaze will settle in the grooves, crevices, and areas with crackled paint.
9. Working quickly so the glaze doesn't have a chance to dry, use a damp rag to remove some of the glaze. Continue wiping until you obtain the softness and contrast you desire.
10. Repeat steps 8 and 9 to complete all the areas of each bar stool. Let dry.
11. Apply sealer or varnish. ❏

Bedroom Furniture

This bedroom furniture was in good condition, but its white and gold finish was dated. A new color palette was chosen to complement the toile bed linens. Four colors of acrylic craft paint were used to enhance the details and create a floral design on the raised panels of the footboard. Choose a design from a decorative painting project book and paint it yourself. The overall surface was treated with a crackling technique.
Décor designed by Connie Sharp

Supplies

Basecoat & Topcoat – Buff, a latex paint in eggshell sheen

Glaze – Van Dyke Brown, clear glazing medium + colorant mixed to produce a dark brown glaze

Acrylic Craft Paints – Green Umber, Fawn, Primrose Red, Teddy Bear Tan, for painting the design and embellishing the furniture

Crackle medium, for creating the crackling. It's a clear liquid that is available in containers of various sizes, including small bottles and jars, quart cans, and tubs. Look for it at crafts, hardware, and paint stores and home improvement centers.

Chip brushes, for applying glazes and for spattering. Other options for spattering include an **old bristle brush or toothbrush**.

Plastic containers, for mixing the glaze (one for each glaze color)

A plastic fork, for mixing the glaze

Soft cloth rags, for wiping

Spray bottle with water, for dampening rags

Bristle brush and/or paint roller and tray, for applying the basecoat

Sample board for testing the results

Supplies for decorative painting (optional): pattern for floral design of your choice (not provided here), transfer paper, stylus, paint brushes, water container, palette

Sealer or varnish or other finish for final topcoat

Instructions

See the "Procedure for Random Linear Crackling" earlier in this section for details.

1. Remove any metal hardware. Prepare the surfaces for painting.
2. Basecoat the furniture with latex paint.
3. Apply crackle medium to the areas of the surface on which you would like cracks to appear. Allow to dry according to manufacturer's instructions. Put some crackle medium on the sample board.
4. Brush Buff paint over the entire surface, including the areas with dried crackle medium, brushing in a single stroke – **do not** brush back and forth. The heavier you apply the paint, the bigger the cracks will be. Let dry at least 24 hours.
5. Mix the glaze.
6. Working one section at a time, brush glaze on the surface in the direction of the wood grain and into the grooves and crevices. The glaze will settle in the areas with crackled paint.
7. Working quickly so the glaze doesn't have a chance to dry, use a damp rag to remove some of the glaze. Continue wiping until you obtain the softness and contrast you desire.
8. Repeat steps 6 and 7 to complete all the areas of the furniture.
9. Use the acrylic craft paints to emphasize details of the furniture, using the photo as a guide.
10. Transfer and paint a design of your choice on the footboard. Let dry.
11. Apply several coats of sealer or varnish to protect the painting. Let dry between coats. Replace the hardware. ❑

Weathered Kitchen Island

The distressed turquoise finish of the island makes it the focal point in this green and white kitchen.
Décor designed by Andrea Costa

Supplies

Basecoat & Topcoat – Turquoise Powder, a latex paint in eggshell sheen

Second Paint Color – Moonlight White, a latex paint in eggshell sheen

Glazes – Van Dyke Brown and Teal, clear glazing medium + colorants to create the two colors of glazes

Crackle medium, for creating the crackling. It's a clear liquid that is available in containers of various sizes, including small bottles and jars, quart cans, and tubs. Look for it at crafts, hardware, and paint stores and home improvement centers.

Chip brushes, for applying glazes and for spattering. Other options for spattering include a **stiff bristle brush or toothbrush**.

Plastic containers, for mixing the glaze (one for each glaze color)

A plastic fork, for mixing the glaze

Soft cloth rags, for wiping

Spray bottle with water, for dampening rags

Bristle brush and/or paint roller and tray, for applying the basecoat

Sample board for testing the results

Sealer or varnish for final protective coat

Instructions

Follow the steps in the "Procedure for Two-Color Crackling" earlier in this section. ❑

Closeup of Cabinet

Entry Stairway

In this impressive foyer, the balustrade (railing), central baluster, column bases, and column capitals are crackled. The balusters (spindles) are striae glaze antiqued, and the column shafts are chamois stippled. The colors chosen complement the marble floor. The variety of techniques used in this one area create a stunning effect, softening and warming this large area.

Railing Close-up

Entry Stairway, continued

Balustrade & Central Baluster

Supplies

Basecoat & Topcoat – Bittersweet Chocolate, a latex paint in eggshell sheen

Other Paint Colors – Mystic Gold, Mayflower Red, latex paints in eggshell sheen

Glaze – Black, clear glazing medium + colorant to produce a black glaze

Crackle medium, for creating the crackling. It's a clear liquid that is available in containers of various sizes, including small bottles and jars, quart cans, and tubs. Look for it at crafts, hardware, and paint stores and home improvement centers.

Chip brushes, for applying glazes and for spattering. Other options for spattering include an **old bristle brush or toothbrush.**

Plastic containers, for mixing the glaze (one for each glaze color)

A plastic fork, for mixing the glaze

Soft cloth rags, for wiping

Spray bottle with water, for dampening rags

Bristle brush and/or paint roller and tray, for applying the basecoat

Sample board for testing the results

Sealer or varnish for final protective coat

Instructions

Follow the steps in the "Procedure for Two-Color Crackling" earlier in this section. ❏

Balusters (Spindles)

Supplies

Basecoat – Mystic Gold, a latex paint in eggshell sheen

Glaze – Burnt Umber, clear glazing medium + colorant to produce a dark brown glaze

Chip brushes or flat paint brushes in a variety of sizes, for applying glaze and creating striae effect

Plastic containers, for mixing the glaze (one for each glaze color)

A plastic fork, for mixing the glaze

Soft cloth rags, for wiping

Spray bottle with water, for dampening rags

Bristle brush and/or paint roller and tray, for applying the basecoat

Sample board for testing results

Instructions

Follow the steps in the "Procedure for Striae Glaze Antiquing" earlier in this book. ❏

Column Capitals & Bases

Supplies

Basecoat & Topcoat – Bittersweet Chocolate, a latex paint in eggshell sheen

Additional Paint Colors – Mystic Gold, Leather Red, latex paint in eggshell sheen

Glaze – Black, clear glazing medium + colorant to create a black glaze

Crackle medium, for creating the crackling. It's a clear liquid that is available in containers of various sizes, including small bottles and jars, quart cans, and tubs. Look for it at crafts, hardware, and paint stores and home improvement centers.

Plastic containers, for mixing the glaze (one for each glaze color)

A plastic fork, for mixing the glaze

Soft cloth rags, for wiping

Spray bottle with water, for dampening rags

Bristle brush and/or paint roller and tray, for applying the basecoat

Sample board for testing the results

Instructions

Follow the steps in the "Procedure for Two-Color Crackling" earlier in this section. ❏

Office Cabinets

Rich color and texture make this workspace inviting. Beadboard panels, installed above the desk top and at the backs of the shelves, add dimension to the formerly flat wall. Rustic colors chosen for the cabinet finishes soften the look of the space and contrast with its high-tech functionality.
Décor designed by Erin Stephenson

Supplies for Beadboard (Striae)

Basecoat – Log Cabin, latex paint in eggshell sheen

Glaze – Van Dyke Brown, clear glazing medium + colorant to produce a dark brown glaze

Supplies for Cabinets

Basecoat and Topcoat – Maple Leaf Red, a latex paint in eggshell sheen

Second Paint Color – Buff, a latex paint in eggshell sheen

Glaze – Van Dyke Brown, clear glazing medium + colorant to produce a dark brown glaze

Crackle medium, for creating the crackling. It's a clear liquid that is available in containers of various sizes, including small bottles and jars, quart cans, and tubs. Look for it at crafts, hardware, and paint stores and home improvement centers.

Chip brushes, for applying glazes and for spattering. Other options for spattering include an **old bristle brush or toothbrush.**

Plastic containers, for mixing the glaze

A plastic fork, for mixing the glaze

Soft cloth rags, for wiping

Spray bottle with water, for dampening rags

Bristle brush and/or paint roller and tray, for applying the basecoat

2 sample boards for testing the results

Sealer or varnish for final protective coat

Instructions

Beadboard
1. Prepare the surfaces for painting. Tape off areas you don't want to paint. Use a drop cloth to protect the floor and adjacent surfaces.
2. Basecoat the beadboard with Log Cabin.
3. Mix the glaze.
4. Working one section of the beadboard at a time, brush glaze on the surface in the direction of the wood grain. The glaze will settle in the grooves and crevices.
5. Working quickly so the glaze doesn't have a chance to dry, use a damp rag to remove some of the glaze from raised areas. Continue wiping until you obtain the softness and contrast you desire.
6. Repeat to complete all the areas. Let dry.

Cabinets
See the "Procedure for Two-Color Crackling" earlier in this section for details.
1. Remove any hardware. Basecoat the cabinets with the red paint. Allow to dry.
2. Randomly apply areas of Buff to the cabinets where you want this color to show through. Allow to dry according to manufacturer's instructions.
3. Brush crackle medium over the cabinet surfaces. Let dry.
4. Brush a coat of Red paint over all the cabinet surfaces in the direction of the wood grain following the stiles and rails. The heavier you apply the paint, the bigger the cracks will be. Let dry at least 24 hours.
5. *Option:* "Erase" some of the crackling by re-painting areas randomly with the Red color. Let dry 24 hours.
6. Mix the glaze.
7. Working one section of the cabinets at a time, brush glaze on the surface in the direction of the wood grain. The glaze will settle in the grooves, crevices, and areas with crackled paint.
8. Repeat step 7 to complete all the areas. Let dry.
9. Seal or varnish.
10. Replace the hardware. ❏

Colorways

Here are other color options. Create your own look by making your own sample boards using your home décor colors.

Colorway 1
Basecoat – Putnam Ivory
Topcoat – Putnam Ivory
Glaze – Raw Umber

Colorway 2 (bottom left)
Basecoat – Tea Chest
Topcoat – White
Glaze – Raw Umber

Colorway 3 (bottom right)
Basecoat – Chili Pepper
Topcoat – Mystic Gold
Glaze – Van Dyke Brown

Colorway 4 (top left)
Basecoat – Cobalt
Topcoat – Little Boy Blue
Glaze – Chambray

Colorway 5 (top right)
Basecoat – Salisbury Green
Additional Colors – Olive,
Golden Tan
Topcoat – Salisbury Green
Glaze – Green Umber

Colorway 6
Basecoat – Florida Keys
Topcoat – Antiguan Blue
Glaze – Medium Gray

Distressed Edging

You can create a rubbed, aged, distressed look without any sanding at all! The technique is amazingly simple. Paint the surface the chosen color. Where you want the surface to look worn from constant rubbing and wear, paint another color that would represent the underneath color. This color gives the appearance that a previous paint color or bare wood is showing through worn spots, when in fact it is painted on top.

Since no sanding is required, there's no dust and no mess, and the original surface isn't altered. Glazing (antiquing) the piece softens the colors and imparts an aged look.

Painting the edges of a door with the flat edge of a foam brush gives the impression of age and wear.

Black Entry Cabinets

A weathered, distressed painted finish makes a focal point of this built-in cabinet. These cabinets are located in the back entry area, adjacent to the mudroom. See page 79 for the full view photo of this area.

Décor designed by Andrea Costa

Supplies

Basecoat – Universal Black, a latex paint with eggshell sheen

Distressing Color – Metallic Bronze, an acrylic craft paint to apply to edges of cabinet

Glaze – Dark Brown, clear glazing medium + Brown paint mixed to produce a dark brown glaze

Foam brush for applying the distressing color

Chip brushes or flat paint brushes in a variety of sizes, for applying glaze

Plastic containers, for mixing the glaze (one for each glaze color)

A plastic fork, for mixing the glaze

Soft cloth rags, for wiping

Spray bottle with water, for dampening rags

Bristle brush and/or paint roller and tray, for applying the basecoat

Sample board for testing results

Sealer or varnish for final protective coat

Instructions

See the "Procedure for Cabinet Doors" in the section on Striae Glaze Antiquing for details.

1. Remove the hardware. Prepare the cabinets for painting. Tape off trim and walls. Protect the floor and adjacent surfaces.
2. Basecoat with Universal Black, applying as many coats as needed to achieve even, opaque coverage. Let dry between coats.
3. Mix the glaze.
4. Working one cabinet door at a time, brush the glaze on the surface in the direction of the wood grain.
5. Working quickly so the glaze doesn't have a chance to dry, use a damp rag to remove some of the glaze. Continue wiping until you obtain the softness and contrast you desire. Remove most of the glaze from the distressed areas.
6. Repeat steps 4 and 5 to complete both the doors.
7. Load the beveled edge of the foam brush with Metallic Bronze. Lightly stroke the raised parts of the door trim. Let dry.
8. Apply sealer or varnish. Replace the hardware. ❏

Black Hutch

Before finishing, this built-in hutch was the same wood tone as the mantle. The distressed painted finish gives the hutch the look of antique furniture and makes the remaining wood and stone elements in the room stand out. Keeping the original wood finish in the cabinet interior helps maintain the harmony of the color palette. Using bronze highlighting on the edges creates the worn look.

Décor designed by Andrea Costa

Supplies

Basecoat – Universal Black, a latex paint with eggshell sheen

Distressing Color – Old World Bronze, an acrylic craft paint to apply to edges of cabinet

Glaze – Dark Brown, clear glazing medium + Brown paint mixed to produce a dark brown glaze

Foam brush for applying the distressing color

Chip brushes or flat paint brushes in a variety of sizes, for applying glaze

Plastic containers, for mixing the glaze (one for each glaze color)

A plastic fork, for mixing the glaze

Soft cloth rags, for wiping

Spray bottle with water, for dampening rags

Bristle brush and/or paint roller and tray, for applying the basecoat

Sample board for testing results

Sealer or varnish for final protective coat

Instructions

See the "Procedure for Cabinet Doors" earlier in the section on Striae Glaze Antiquing for details.

1. Remove the hardware. Prepare the hutch for painting. Tape off trim and walls. Protect the floor and adjacent areas.

2. Basecoat with Universal Black, applying as many coats as needed to achieve even, opaque coverage. Let dry between coats.

3. Mix the glaze.

4. Working one cabinet door at a time, brush the glaze on the surface in the direction of the wood grain.

5. Working quickly so the glaze doesn't have a chance to dry, use a damp rag to remove some of the glaze. Continue wiping until you obtain the softness and contrast you desire. Remove most of the glaze from the distressed areas.

6. Repeat steps 4 and 5 to complete the doors.

7. Load the beveled edge of the foam brush with Old World Bronze. Lightly stroke the edges of the doors and drawers for a worn look. The application should be random rather than uniform. Allow to dry.

8. Apply sealer or varnish. Replace the hardware. ❏

Before

Brush Stippling

Stippling can be used to soften a strong color by toning it down with a glaze topcoat. Both sponging and stippling are created by pouncing a tool on a glaze coated surface. Stippling is done with a brush. Sponging adds color to a surface with a natural sea sponge or cellulose sponge, providing a mottled look.

For stippling, glaze is applied over a painted surface with a brush, pouncing it to remove some of the glaze and creating a refined imprint of color. The more the glaze is worked, the softer it will appear. The overall impression of brush stippling can resemble the look of suede or cotton, and stippling can give a new surface a gently aged look. This blended finish requires a consistent touch and quality products.

When stippling walls, it is a good idea to recruit a partner to help – one partner can apply the glaze, the other can do the stippling. This division of labor gives you enough time to adequately manipulate the glaze before it dries, thus avoiding lap lines of glaze.

Pictured right: Soft stippling enhances and adds texture to a bathroom wall. The wall was painted a medium green color. It was stippled with a green umber glaze and a burnt umber glaze.

Basic Supplies

Paints

Latex paint, eggshell sheen is needed to basecoat the wall or the furniture

Glaze

Clear glazing medium, to mix with a colorant to make an antiquing glaze

Colorant can be paint, a colored glaze or universal tint. It is mixed with the clear glazing medium to create the antiquing glaze.

Texturing Tools

Stipple brushes or stencil brushes, for pouncing glaze. Stencil brushes can be used in small areas and stipple brushes in large areas.

Chip brushes or flat paint brushes in a variety of sizes, for applying glaze

Other Supplies

Plastic containers, for mixing the glaze (one for each glaze color)

A plastic fork, for mixing the glaze

Painter's tape, for protecting trim

Bristle brush and/or paint roller and tray, for applying the basecoat

Paper towels, for wiping brushes

Pictured above, top row: Two stipple brushes
Bottom row: Two chip brushes, two stencil brushes

Procedure for One-Color Stippling

On walls, work one 2-ft. x 2-ft. section at a time. Work at an angle from top to bottom.

Prepare

1. Prepare the walls for painting, following the guidelines for cleaning, repairing, and priming in the section on Surface Preparation.
2. Tape off any molding or trim with painter's masking tape to protect them.
3. Use drop cloths to protect the floor or any adjacent surfaces.
4. If you're planning to paint the ceiling, paint it before you paint the walls.

Basecoat

5. The basecoat is the first color applied to the surface and is the foundation of your creative finish. Apply the basecoat with a brush, short-nap roller, or a paint sprayer. Apply as many coats as needed to achieve even, opaque coverage. Let dry between coats.

Mix the Glaze

6. Pour some glazing medium in a plastic tub or other container. Add colorant to the container, a few drops at a time. Mix to combine. (I like to use a plastic fork.) Continue to stir until the glaze color is thoroughly mixed.

Apply Glaze

7. Use a large, flat bristle brush (such as a chip brush) to apply crosshatch strokes of glaze to a section of the basecoated surface. Begin about one foot away from any edges or corners. **(photo 1)**

Pounce

8. While the glaze is still wet, use a pouncing motion with a stipple brush to move the glaze. Start in the center of the glazed area and pouncing outward. **(photo 2)**

9. Keep pouncing to distribute and smooth the glaze, working out to the edges of area. **(photo 3)** You do not want to see brush marks, so pounce – do not rub. Keep spreading the glaze with the brush until all the edges of the glazed section are soft and the stipple brush appears to be empty.

Apply More Glaze

10. Apply more glaze about one foot away from the area that was just pounced. Pounce again, starting in the center of the glazed area and working outward, blending gently into the adjacent wet edge. Wipe the stipple brush occasionally on a paper towel to remove excess glaze.

11. Repeat the procedure until the entire surface has been glazed and pounced.

Procedure for Two-Color Stippling

First basecoat the walls and mix your glaze colors.

Apply Glaze

1. Apply the first color of glaze, using crosshatch strokes. Leave some empty spaces between the strokes for the second glaze color.
2. While the first color of glaze is still wet, apply the second color, using crosshatch strokes, between the crosshatch strokes of the first color. **(photo 1)**

Pounce

3. While the glazes are still wet, use a pouncing motion with a stipple brush to move the glazes and blend the colors, starting in the center of the glazed area and pouncing outward from the center. **(photo 2)**
4. Continue pouncing to work color out to the edges of the area and smooth the glaze. **(photo 3)** ❏

Bedroom Walls

These softly textured bedroom walls were stippled with one glaze color. The stippling adds a depth of color and textural interest that is not possible with simply painted walls.

Décor designed by Connie Sharp

Supplies

Basecoat – Jalapeno Pepper a latex paint in an eggshell sheen to paint the walls.

Glaze – Earth Brown, clear glazing medium + colorant to produce a medium brown glaze

Stipple brushes for pouncing glaze

Chip brushes or flat paint brushes in a variety of sizes, for applying glaze

Plastic containers, for mixing the glaze (one for each glaze color)

A plastic fork, for mixing the glaze

Painter's masking tape, for protecting trim

Bristle brush and/or paint roller and tray, for applying the basecoat

Paper towels, for wiping brushes

Sample board, to test color results

Instructions

Follow the "Procedure for One-Color Stippling" earlier in this section.

1. Prepare the walls for painting. Tape off any molding or trim with painter's masking tape to protect them. Use drop cloths to protect the floor or any adjacent surfaces.
2. Basecoat the walls with Jalapeno Pepper. Apply as many coats as needed to achieve even, opaque coverage. Let dry between coats. Paint a sample board.

3. Mix the glaze. Brush some on the sample board and pounce. Let dry. Adjust the glaze color as needed.

4. Working one section at a time, apply crosshatch strokes of glaze to a section of a wall, beginning about 1 foot away from any edges or corners.

5. While the glaze is still wet, use a pouncing motion with a stipple brush to move the glaze, starting in the center of the glazed area and pouncing outward from the center.

6. Apply more glaze about 1 foot away from the area that was just pounced. Pounce again, starting in the center of the glazed area and working outward, blending gently into the adjacent wet edge. Wipe the brush occasionally on a paper towel to remove excess glaze. Repeat the procedure until the entire surface has been glazed and pounced. Let dry. ❑

Master Bath Columns

Two glaze colors give these columns the look of marble. Varying the intensity of the
glaze and the placement add to the authentic look.

Supplies

Basecoat – Neutral White, a latex paint in eggshell
sheen for painting columns

Glazes – Raw Umber, Mushroom clear glazing
medium + colorant to create the two glaze colors

Acrylic Craft Paint – Metallic Gold, for trim color

Stipple brushes for pouncing glaze

Chip brushes or flat paint brushes in a variety of sizes,
for applying glaze

Plastic containers, for mixing the glaze (one for each
glaze color)

A plastic fork, for mixing the glaze

Painter's tape, for protecting trim

Bristle brush and/or paint roller and tray, for applying
the basecoat

Paper towels, for wiping brushes

Sample board, to test color results

Instructions

*Follow the "Procedure for Two-Color Stippling" earlier in
this section.*

1. Prepare the columns for painting. Tape off the trim
   with painter's masking tape to protect it. Use drop
   cloths to protect the floor, furniture, and fixtures.
2. Basecoat the columns with Neutral White. Apply as
   many coats as needed to achieve even, opaque coverage. Let dry between coats. Paint a sample board.
3. Mix the glazes. Brush some of each on the sample
   board and pounce. Let dry. Adjust the glaze colors as
   needed.
4. Working one area at a time, apply the first glaze color,
   using crosshatch strokes. Leave some empty spaces
   between the strokes for the second glaze color. While
   the first color of glaze is still wet, apply the second
   color, using crosshatch strokes, between the crosshatch strokes of the first color.
5. While the glazes are still wet, use a pouncing motion
   with a stipple brush to move the glazes and blend the
   colors. Continue pouncing to work color out to the
   edges of the area.
6. Apply more glazes in an adjacent area. Pounce again,
   starting in the center of the glazed area and working
   outward, blending gently into the adjacent wet edge.
   Wipe the brush occasionally on a paper towel to
   remove excess glaze. Repeat the procedure until the
   entire surface has been glazed and pounced. Let dry.
   Remove the tape.
7. Paint the capital and the adjacent trim on the base
   with Metallic Gold. Let dry. ❑

Empire Style Sofa

Stippling can also be used to create fine texture on furniture, like this wood-frame sofa. Random areas are stippled with a light colored acrylic paint for an aged look. On fabric-covered furniture pieces, it's best to finish the frame, then upholster.

Supplies

Basecoat – Bittersweet Chocolate to paint the frame

Glaze – Espresso

Acrylic Craft Paint – Warm White, for the aged stippling

Stipple brushes or stencil brushes, for pouncing white paint

Chip brushes or flat paint brushes in a variety of sizes, for applying glaze

Plastic containers, for mixing the glaze (one for each glaze color)

A plastic fork, for mixing the glaze

Painter's tape, for protecting trim

Bristle brush and/or paint roller and tray, for applying the basecoat

Paper towels, for wiping brushes

Sample board, to test color results

Sealer or varnish for final protective coat

Instructions

Follow the "Procedure for One-Color Stippling" earlier in this section.

1. Prepare the sofa frame for painting. Use drop cloths to protect the floor.
2. Basecoat the sofa frame with Bittersweet Chocolate. Apply as many coats as needed to achieve even, opaque coverage. Let dry between coats. Paint a sample board.
3. Mix the glaze. Brush some on the sample board and pounce. Let dry. Adjust the glaze color as needed.
4. Apply glaze to the sofa frame using the "Striae Glaze Antiquing" procedure. Let dry.
5. Randomly pounce areas with the white acrylic paint to create the aged look. Allow to dry.
6. Apply sealer or varnish. ❑

Colorways

Here are other options for colors. Do your own sample boards with your home décor colors for your own custom look.

Colorway 1
Basecoat – Spice Tan
Glaze – Toffee Orange

Colorway 2
Basecoat – Florida Keys
Glaze – Nantucket Navy

Colorway 3
Basecoat – White
Glaze – Earth Brown

Colorway 4
Basecoat – Mellow Yellow
Glazes – Sunflower, Asphaltum

Colorway 5
Basecoat – Putnam Ivory
Glazes – Mushroom, Russet

Colorway 6
Basecoat – Antiguan
Glaze – Raw Umber

Chamois Stippling

Different types of paint tools offer a multitude of effects that imitate nature. Two of these are the chamois tool, which has pieces of chamois cloth attached to a handle, and the chamois mitt, which has pieces of chamois cloth attached to the face of a mitt. The tools can be used to produce textured effects with the look of top grain leather or the more organic look of stone. The random pattern produced by pouncing with the tool or mitt is very forgiving on imperfect surfaces. *Sponging,* usually done with a sponge is the procedure of *pouncing* a sponge on the surface. Stippling is done the same way – but it is done with a chamois tool or mitt – creating a much more interesting finish.

Basic Supplies

Paints
Latex paint, eggshell sheen is needed to basecoat the wall or the furniture

Glaze
Clear glazing medium, to mix with a colorant to make an antiquing glaze

Colorant can be paint, a colored glaze or universal tint. It is mixed with the clear glazing medium to create the glaze.

Texturing Tools
Chamois mitt or chamois tool, for producing texture

Other Supplies
Disposable foam plate, to use as a palette

Squeeze bottles, for holding glaze

Plastic containers, for mixing the glaze (one for each glaze color)

A plastic fork, for mixing the glaze

Painter's masking tape, for protecting trim

Bristle brush and/or paint roller and tray, for applying the basecoat

Pictured clockwise from top left: Chamois mitt, glazes in squeeze bottles, disposable plate, chamois tool

Procedure for Chamois Stippling

Work in small sections so you can manipulate the glaze before it dries. These examples show how to use a chamois mitt.

Prepare

1. Prepare the surface for painting, following the guidelines for cleaning, repairing, and priming in the section on "Surface Preparation."
2. Tape off any molding or trim with painter's tape to protect them.
3. Use drop cloths to protect the floor or any adjacent surfaces.
4. If you're working on walls and you're planning to paint the ceiling, paint it before you paint the walls.

Basecoat

5. Use an eggshell sheen paint. Apply the basecoat with a brush or a short-nap roller. Apply as many coats as needed to achieve even, opaque coverage. Let dry between coats.

Mix the Glaze

6. Add colorant to glazing medium and mix thoroughly to combine. Put tinted glaze in a squeeze bottle.

Load the Tool

7. Dampen the mitt or tool with water to soften it.
8. Squirt some glaze onto a foam plate in a spiral pattern. **(photo 1)**
9. Load the mitt by pressing it into the glaze on the plate. **(photo 2)**

Pounce the Surface

10. Press the glaze-loaded tool on to the surface with a pouncing motion. Rotate your hand with each stroke to give a random pattern to the finish. TIP: Use the same motion you use to open and close a door knob. **(photo 3)**

Two-Color Option

11. To incorporate more than one color, mix two glaze colors and use two different plates, one for each glaze color. **(photo 4)**
12. Dip the dampened chamois mitt (or tool) in one color glaze and pounce on the surface, leaving some blank spaces for the second color.
13. Dip the same mitt into the second color.
14. Apply the second color to surface, filling the blank spaces and overlapping first color. As you pounce, the colors will blend into each other along the edges. **(photo 5)**

Continued on page 98

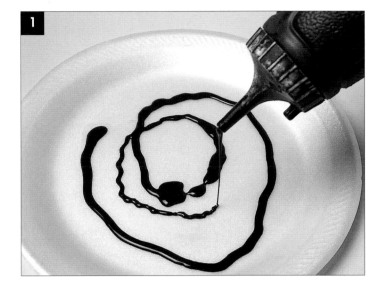

Study Walls

Chamois mitt was used to create the leather-like look of these walls. Be sure to work in small sections so you can manipulate the glaze before it dries.

Décor designed by Connie Sharp

Supplies

Basecoat – Red, a latex paint in eggshell sheen

Glazes- Burgundy, Espresso, clear glazing medium + colorants to mix the two glaze colors

Chamois mitt or chamois tool, for producing texture

Disposable foam plate, to use as a palette

Squeeze bottles, for holding glaze

Plastic containers, for mixing the glaze (one for each glaze color)

A plastic fork, for mixing the glaze

Painter's masking tape, for protecting trim

Bristle brush and/or paint roller and tray, for applying the basecoat

Sample board to test color results

Hair dryer, for drying the sample board

Instructions

See the "Procedure for Chamois Stippling" earlier in this section.

1. Prepare the walls for painting. Tape off molding and trim with painter's masking tape to protect them. Use drop cloths to protect the floor or any adjacent surface.
2. Basecoat the wall with Red, applying as many coats as needed to achieve even, opaque coverage. Let dry between coats. Paint a sample board. Let dry.
3. Mix the glazes.
4. Put the tinted glazes in squeeze bottles. Squirt each glaze color on a separate foam plate in a spiral pattern.
5. Dampen the mitt with water to soften it. Load the mitt by pressing it into the glaze on the plate.
6. Pounce the mitt on the sample board. Load the mitt with the second glaze color. Pounce on the sample board. Dry with a hair dryer. Adjust the glaze colors as needed.
7. Load the mitt with one glaze color. Pounce the mitt on the walls, leaving some blank spaces for the second color.
8. Dip the same mitt in the second color and apply the second color to surface, filling the blank spaces and overlapping first color. As you pounce, the colors will blend. Continue until all the walls are covered.
9. Let dry. Remove tape. ❏

Entry Columns

Three glaze colors were pounced on the shafts of these columns with a chamois mitt to create the look of stone.

Supplies

Basecoat – Richmond Gold, a latex paint in eggshell sheen for painting columns

Glazes – Raw Umber, Burnt Umber, Green Umber, clear glazing medium + colorants to create the three glaze colors

Chamois mitt or chamois tool, for producing texture

Disposable foam plate, to use as a palette

Squeeze bottles, for holding glaze

Plastic containers, for mixing the glaze (one for each glaze color)

A plastic fork, for mixing the glaze

Painter's masking tape, for protecting trim

Bristle brush and/or paint roller and tray, for applying the basecoat

Sample board to test color results

Hair dryer, for drying the sample board

Instructions

See the "Procedure for Chamois Stippling" earlier in this section.

1. Prepare the column shafts for painting. Mask off the capitals and bases with painter's masking tape to protect them. Use drop cloths to protect the floor or any furniture that's still in the room.
2. Basecoat with Richmond Gold, applying as many coats as needed to achieve even, opaque coverage. Let dry between coats. Paint a sample board. Let dry.
3. Mix the glazes.
4. Put the tinted glazes in squeeze bottles. Squirt the each glaze color on a separate foam plate in a spiral pattern.
5. Dampen the chamois mitt with water to soften it. Load the mitt by pressing it into the glaze on the plate.
6. Pounce the mitt on the sample board. Load the mitt with the second glaze color. Pounce on the sample board, then load the third glaze color and pounce that. Dry with a hair dryer. Adjust the glaze colors as needed.
7. Load the mitt with one glaze color. Pounce the mitt on columns, leaving some blank spaces for the second and third colors.
8. Dip the same mitt in the second color and apply the second color to surface, filling some of the blank spaces and overlapping first color. As you pounce, the colors will blend.
9. Dip the mitt in the third glaze color and pounce on the remaining blank spaces. Continue until all the columns are covered.
10. Let dry. Remove tape. ❏

Colorways

Here are other color options. Create your own look by making your own sample boards using your home décor colors.

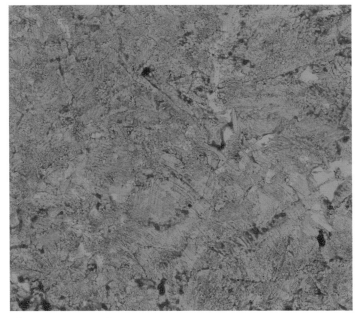

Colorway 1
Basecoat – Richmond Gold
Glaze – Asphaltum

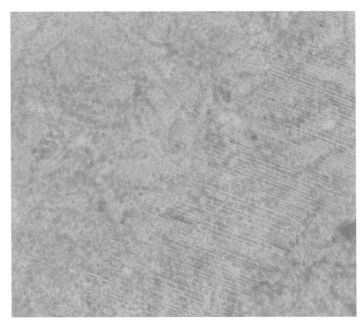

Colorway 2
Basecoat – Beige
Glazes – Earth Brown, Earth Green

Colorway 3
Basecoat – Golden Tan
Glaze – Green Umber

Colorway 4
Basecoat – Fairway Oaks
Glazes – Mahogany, Van Dyke Brown

Colorways

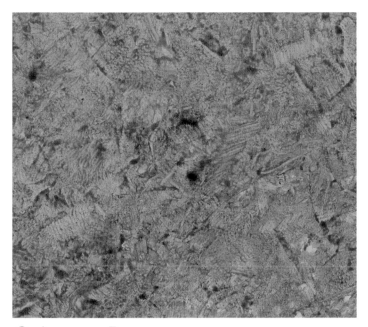

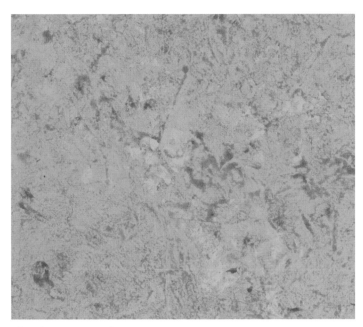

Colorway 5
Basecoat – Gray Horse
Glazes – Burnt Umber, Coffee Brown

Colorway 6
Basecoat – Waterfall
Glaze – Soft Teal

Colorway 7
Basecoat – Red
Glazes – Black Cherry,
       Bittersweet Chocolate

Wood Graining

Wood graining is a painted finish that gives the look of wood to surfaces. It can be applied to doors, cabinets, trim, and furniture. It's an especially effective way to "refinish" a painted door or to create the look of wood on furniture. Using at least two colors of glaze adds depth and realism to this technique.

Basic Supplies

Paints

Latex paint, eggshell sheen is needed to basecoat the wall or the furniture

Glaze

Clear glazing medium, to mix with a colorant to make an antiquing glaze

Colorant can be paint, a colored glaze or universal tint. It is mixed with the clear glazing medium to create the antiquing glaze.

Texturing Tools

Chip brushes, for applying glaze (one for each glaze color) and for smoothing

Wood graining tool – a rocker tool, wood graining roller, or combs

Other Supplies

Plastic containers, for mixing the glaze (one for each glaze color)

A plastic fork, for mixing the glaze

Bristle brush and/or paint roller and tray, for applying the basecoat

Optional: **Stiff bristle brush or toothbrush and latex gloves**, for spattering

Pictured at top: Wood graining roller
Pictured below, left to right: Wood graining rocker tool, two chip brushes

Continued on page 106

Procedure for Wood Graining

These examples use a rocker-type wood graining tool.

Prepare

1. Prepare the surface for painting, following the guidelines for cleaning, repairing, and priming in the section on "Surface Preparation."
2. Use drop cloths to protect the floor or adjacent surfaces.

Basecoat

3. The basecoat is the first color applied to the surface and is the foundation of your creative finish. Apply the basecoat with a brush, short-nap roller, or paint sprayer. Apply as many coats as needed to achieve even, opaque coverage. Let dry between coats.

Mix the Glazes

4. Pour some glazing medium in each of two plastic tubs or other containers.
5. Add colorant to each container, a few drops at a time.
6. Mix to combine with a plastic fork. Continue to stir until the glaze color is consistent.

Apply First Glaze Color

7. Working from the top to the bottom of the piece, apply the first glaze color on the basecoated surface, using a chip brush. Apply glaze in straight, parallel strokes, working from the top to the bottom. Allow space between each row of glaze for the second color of glaze. **(photo 1)**

Apply Second Glaze Color

8. Apply the second color of glaze in the spaces between strokes of the first glaze color. **(photo 2)**

Blend with a Brush

9. Use a chip brush to blend and smooth the glaze colors. **(photo 3)**

Create the Wood Grain

10. Pull the wood graining tool straight through the glaze, from the top of the area to the bottom in one continuous motion, rocking the tool as you move down the wall or the surface. **(photo 4)** Let glaze dry slightly, until tacky.

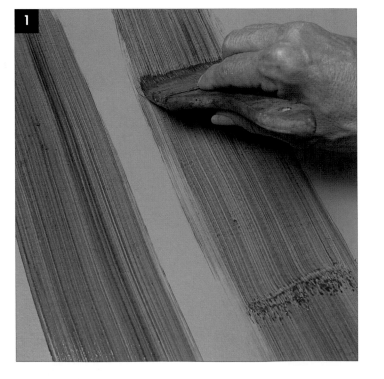

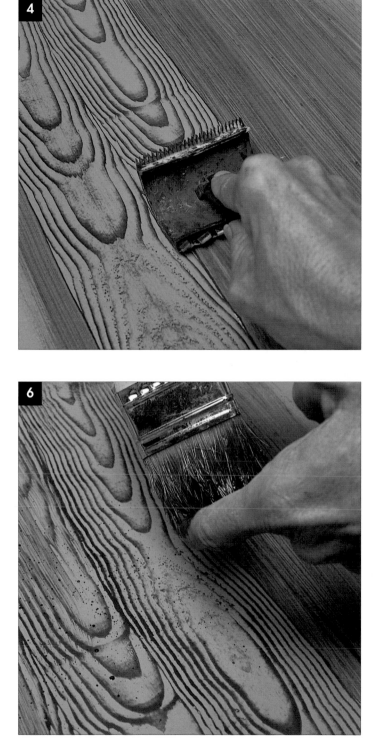

Soften with a Brush

11. Lightly pull the tips of the bristles of a clean chip brush over the texture to soften the lines of the wood graining. **(photo 5)** Let dry.

Spatter

12. Mix dark tint with water to thin it to an inky consistency. (Here, I'm using a chocolate brown.)

13. Load the chip brush, a flat bristle brush, or an old toothbrush with the inky glaze.

14. Pull your finger across the bristles of the brush to spatter dots of glaze across the surface. **(photo 6)** TIP: To keep your hands clean, wear latex gloves.

Bookshelves

These built-in bookshelves have wood graining on the cabinet doors for added interest. The casings of the bookshelves are finished with the striae glaze antiquing technique using the same color. For information on that technique, see the section on Striae Glaze Antiquing earlier in this book.

Supplies

Basecoat – Coppertone, a latex paint in eggshell sheen

Glazes – Raw Umber, Burnt Umber, clear glazing medium + colorants to produce two colors of antiquing glaze

Chip brushes, for applying glaze (one for each glaze color) and for smoothing

Wood graining tool – a rocker tool, wood graining roller, or combs

Plastic containers, for mixing the glaze (one for each glaze color)

A plastic fork, for mixing the glaze

Bristle brush and/or paint roller and tray, for applying the basecoat

Optional: **Stiff bristle brush or toothbrush and latex gloves**, for spattering

Sample board, to test color results

Sealer or varnish for final protective coat

Instructions

See the "Procedure for Wood Graining" earlier in this section.

1. Remove the hardware. Prepare the surfaces for painting.
2. Basecoat the bookshelves with Coppertone. Apply as many coats as needed to achieve even, opaque coverage. Let dry between coats. Paint the sample board.
3. Mix the Raw Umber and Burnt Umber glazes. Try the colors on the sample board. Let dry. Adjust as needed.
4. Apply the striae glazing technique to the casings first. Allow to dry.
5. Working one cabinet door at a time, apply the first glaze color to the raised panel, using a chip brush to make straight, parallel strokes, working from the top to the bottom. Allow space between each row of glaze for the second glaze color.
6. Apply the second color of glaze in the spaces between strokes of the first glaze color.
7. Use a chip brush to blend and smooth the glaze colors.
8. Pull the wood graining tool through the glaze, from the top of the area to the bottom in one continuous motion, rocking the tool as you move it. Let glaze dry slightly, until tacky.
9. Lightly pull the tips of the bristles of a chip brush over the texture to soften the lines of the wood graining.
10. Repeat steps 5 through 9 to complete all the cabinet doors, following the directional pattern of stiles and rails. Let dry.
11. Apply sealer or varnish. Replace hardware. ❏

Door in Kitchen

The wood graining on this formerly painted door was created to coordinate with the wooden kitchen cabinets.

Décor designed by Andrea Costa

Supplies

Basecoat – Camel, a latex paint in eggshell sheen to paint door

Glazes – Raw Umber, Brown, clear glazing medium + colorants to create the two antiquing glaze colors

Chip brushes, for applying glaze (one for each glaze color) and for smoothing

Wood graining tool – a rocker tool, wood graining roller, or combs

Plastic containers, for mixing the glaze (one for each glaze color)

A plastic fork, for mixing the glaze

Bristle brush and/or paint roller and tray, for applying the basecoat

Sample board, to test color results

Sealer or varnish for final protective coat

Instructions

See the "Procedure for Wood Graining" earlier in this section.

1. Remove the hardware. Prepare the door for painting.
2. Basecoat the door with Camel. Apply as many coats as needed to achieve even, opaque coverage. Let dry between coats. Paint the sample board.
3. Mix the Raw Umber and Brown glazes. Try the colors on the sample board. Let dry. Adjust as needed.
4. Use tape to mask off the sections of the door. Working one section at a time, apply the first glaze color, using a chip brush to make straight, parallel strokes. Allow space between each row of glaze for the second glaze color.
5. Apply the second color of glaze in the spaces between strokes of the first glaze color.
6. Use a chip brush to blend and smooth the glaze colors.
7. Pull the wood graining tool through the glaze, from the top of the area to the bottom or one side to the other in one continuous motion, rocking the tool as you move it. Let glaze dry slightly, until tacky.
8. Lightly pull the tips of the bristles of a chip brush over the texture to soften the lines of the wood graining.
9. Repeat steps 4 through 8 to complete all the sections of the door. Let dry. TIP: Do vertical graining first. Allow these areas to dry thoroughly before treating horizontal sections.
10. Apply sealer or varnish. Replace hardware. ❏

Closeup of door

Before

ntinually;

tances ...

Thes. 5:16

Stenciling

Stenciling is a traditional surface decorating technique where paint is applied through openings in a material that is resistant to paint to create a design. It's a great way to create borders with repeating designs, embellish corners, or place words on walls.
Pre-cut stencils are available at crafts and home improvement centers or on-line in a huge array of designs (including alphabets), or you can create and cut your own custom designs from stencil blank material.

Basic Supplies

Paints

Latex paint, eggshell sheen is needed to basecoat the wall or the furniture

Stencil paint or acrylic craft paint are needed to do the stenciling

Tools & Other Supplies

Stencil – You can use pre-cut stencils or cut your own with stencil blank material, using a **craft knife**

Stencil brushes, for applying paint

Disposable foam plate or palette, for holding stenciling paint

Paper towels, for blotting brushes

Painter's tape, for creating simple borders and holding stencils in place on surfaces

Burnisher, such as a plastic putty knife, plastic spatula, or credit card

Measuring tape or yardstick, for measuring

Laser level or bubble level as a guide to align designs

Pictured above, clockwise from top left: Painter's tape, plastic putty knife, disposable plate, paper towel, stencil, three stencil brushes in various sizes

Procedure for Stenciling

This project is an example of how to use a single stencil to create interest in a small and non-descript space. A simple line connects a delicate design that is used to embellish each corner of the walls and frame the acessories.
Décor designed by Erin Stephenson

Prepare

1. Prepare the surface for painting, following the guidelines for cleaning, repairing, and priming in the section on "Surface Preparation."
2. Use drop cloths to protect the floor and adjacent surfaces.

Basecoat

3. Paint the basecoat with a brush, short-nap roller, or paint sprayer. Apply as many coats as needed to achieve even, opaque coverage. Let dry between coats.

Determine the Placement

4. Decide where you want the stenciled designs to be placed. Depending on the space and type of design, you may wish to use the stencil to make paper samples of the design and tape them to the wall, moving them around until you determine the correct placement.
5. Use masking tape to mark off lines for a border and the positioning of the corner design. Place the masking tape along one side and along the top to align the corner design.
6. Use a plastic spatula or a credit card to burnish the tape so you won't have any paint run-unders. **(photo 1)**

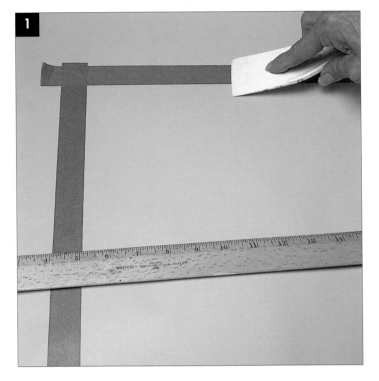

Position the Stencil

7. Position the stencil for the corner motif and tape in place. Tape the stencil only at top. **(photo 2)**
8. Pull up the tape to clear the area of the stencil motif. **(photo 3)** Retape the overlay to secure.

Load the Brush

9. Squeeze some paint on a disposable plate. Load a stencil brush by dipping the tips of the bristles in the paint. **(photo 4)**
10. Swirl the brush on another area of the plate to remove excess paint and work the paint into the bristles. **(photo 5)**
11. Blot excess paint on the side of the brush on a paper towel. **(photo 6)**

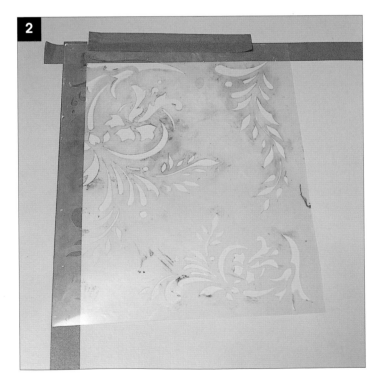

Continued on next page

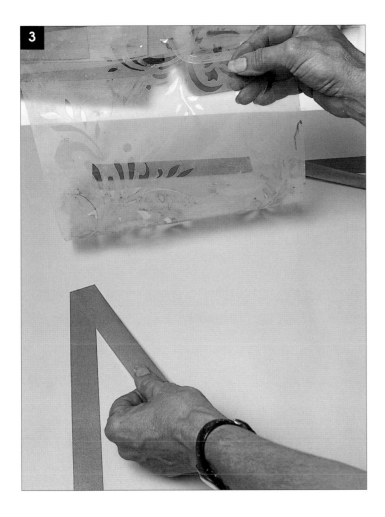

Stencil

12. Pounce the brush in the cut openings of the stencil to paint the design. **(photo 7)** Re-load the brush as needed to complete the stenciled design. Remove the stencil. Let dry.

Tape the Border

13. Press the tape to the wall where the top of the border will be. Using the plastic putty knife, tear off the end of the tape. **(photo 8)**
14. Add another piece of tape parallel to the first piece, leaving a space between the pieces that is the width of the border you wish to create. **(photo 9)**
15. Place a piece of tape across the end of the border. **(photo 10)** Burnish the tape to secure it to the wall.

Stencil the Border

16. Re-load stencil brush, blot it, and pounce color into the opening between tape pieces. **(photo 11)**
17. Carefully remove the tape and allow to dry completely. **(photo 12)**

Continued on pages 116 & 117

Words on Walls

Stenciled messages or mottoes can add an interesting finishing touch to stippled, sponged, striae glazed, or crackled walls. You can buy pre-cut stencils of sayings or create your own with alphabet stencils.

Décor designed by Andrea Costa

Supplies

Stencil Paint – Black for stenciling the words

Alphabet stencil, for the words

Stencil brushes, for applying paint

Disposable foam plate or palette, for holding stenciling paint

Paper towels, for blotting brushes

Painter's masking tape, for creating simple borders and holding stencils in place on surfaces

Burnisher, such as a plastic putty knife, plastic spatula, or credit card

Measuring tape or yardstick, for measuring

Laser level or bubble level for marking guidelines

Instructions

See the "Procedure for Stenciling" at the beginning of this section.

1. Prepare the surface for painting.
2. Apply your chosen finish to the wall.
3. Determine the placement of the stenciled designs.
4. Position the stencil and tape in place.
5. Squeeze some paint on a disposable plate. Load the stencil brush and blot.
6. Stencil the design. Re-load the brush and move the stencil as needed. Let dry. ❏

SING...

like nobody's

listening.

Feathers on Walls

Random repetition of a single motif provides a simple, effective embellishment to walls. Variation is achieved by turning the stencil – rotating and/or reversing the design. Using partial motifs at edges and corners is a way of creating continuity and flow of the design.

Supplies

Stencil Paint – Antique Gold and Antique Copper for the stencil design

Feather design stencil, pre-cut design to stencil on walls

Stencil brushes, for applying paint

Disposable foam plate or palette, for holding stenciling paint

Paper towels, for blotting brushes

Instructions

See the "Procedure for Stenciling" at the beginning of this section.

1. Prepare the surface for painting.
2. Apply your chosen finish to the wall.
3. Determine the placement of the stenciled designs.
4. Position the stencil and tape in place.
5. Squeeze some paint on a disposable plate. Load the stencil brush and blot.
6. Stencil the design. Re-load the brush and move the stencil as needed. Let dry. ❑

Tissue Paper Texturing

This technique sandwiches crumpled tissue paper between two coats of paint to add dimensional texture to a surface. The effect has been said to resemble a hide of leather, a wilted tobacco leaf, or hammered metal. The texture of the tissue makes the technique a good choice for covering uneven or damaged surfaces. It can be used to cover walls or as a textural accent on accessories such as lampshades or candle holders.
Varying the colors of tissue and paint offers endless possibilities. Preparation is minimal. If the surface is raw wood or is already covered with latex paint, additional basecoating is not required.

Pictured above, left to right: 4" paint roller, squeeze bottle for glaze, latex gloves, and (underneath) white tissue paper.

Basic Supplies

Paints

Latex paint, eggshell sheen This is both the basecoat and the glue that holds the tissue to the surface. *Option:* For a more translucent look, use a mixture of equal amounts of glazing medium and paint.

Glaze

Clear glazing medium, to mix with the colorant to create the antiquing glaze

Colorants, paints or colored glazes for tinting the glazing medium

Tools & Other Supplies

Tissue paper – Can be white or colored, and since you will be crumpling it before it is applied to the surface, it doesn't have to be new or smooth. Calculate how much you will need to cover the entire area that you will be texturing. Allow a little extra for overlapping.

4" paint roller and paint tray, for applying paint

Squeeze bottle, for holding glaze

Latex gloves, to protect your hands when applying the glaze

Painter's masking tape, to protect areas you don't wish to texture

Craft knife and metal straight edge, for removing tape

For a more translucent look like this shade, start with a white lampshade. Apply the tissue using a mixture of equal amounts of glazing medium and gold paint. Allow two days to cure. (Glaze takes longer to dry than paint.) Rub with a soft metallic glaze to bring out the texture.

Procedure for Tissue Paper Texturing

Prepare the Surface

1. Tape off areas of the surface you are decorating that you aren't texturing or adjacent areas you wish to protect, such as trim.

Prepare the Paper

2. Tear pieces of tissue paper into pieces of manageable size (not larger than about 18" x 18"). Do not leave any straight or cut edges – all the edges should be irregular, ragged, and torn. **(photo 1)** The size of the pieces depends on the size of the area you are planning to cover. For a wall, you would tear the pieces into rough 12" or 18" squares. For smaller projects, such as a lampshade, you might use 4" to 6" pieces. Tear enough pieces to cover the space you are going to finish.
3. Crumple the torn pieces. **(photo 2)**
4. Smooth the pieces so they retain some wrinkles but are somewhat flat.

Paint the Surface

5. Using a roller, apply a medium, thick coat of eggshell sheen latex paint to the surface. Use plenty – this paint is both basecoat and glue. **(photo 3)** If you are covering a large area, such as a wall, work in one small area at a time so you'll have time to apply the paper before the paint dries.

Position the Paper Pieces

6. While the paint is still wet, lay the wrinkled tissue piece over the wet paint, using your hands to press the tissue to the surface. **(photo 4)** Do not smooth out all the wrinkles – the wrinkles create the texture.
7. Reload the roller with paint and roll over the paper piece, working from the center of the tissue outward to press out the air bubbles. **(photo 5)** Be sure to use plenty of paint, and don't press too hard – the idea is to flatten but not crush the tissue. Too much pressure can cause the tissue to stretch or tear.
8. Move to another area, applying paint, then tissue, then paint, until the entire surface is covered. Make sure the edges of the tissue overlap. Let dry completely, allowing 24 to 48 hours.

Glaze

9. Put tinted glaze in a squeeze bottle, and put on latex gloves. Squeeze some glaze into your hand (like you would hand lotion). **(photo 6)**
10. Use your gloved hands to rub the glaze on the surface in all directions, allowing the glaze to settle in the wrinkles of the tissue, enhancing the texture. **(photo 7)** TIP: Using circular scrubbing motions – clockwise and counterclockwise – will help distribute the glaze in all the crevices. Allow to dry completely.

Glaze Again *Optional*

11. Multiple glaze colors can be used. Alternate the application of each color. **(photo 8)** Blend the edges of the colors with your hands to soften the transition of the different tones.
12. Since the paint is so thick, allow to dry at least 24-48 hours.

Remove the Tape

13. Remove any tape. TIP: To avoid tearing the tissue and disrupting the finish, score the edges along the taped line, using a craft knife and metal straight edge, before pulling off the tape.

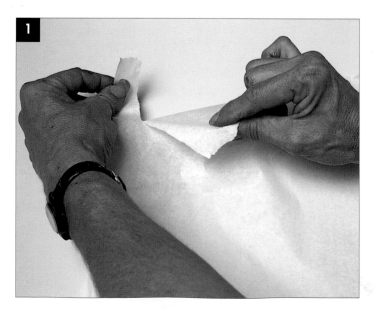

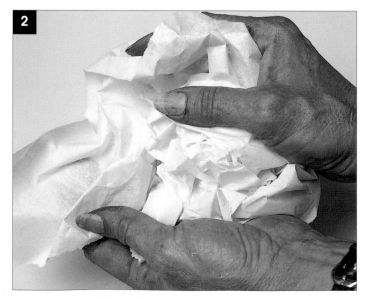

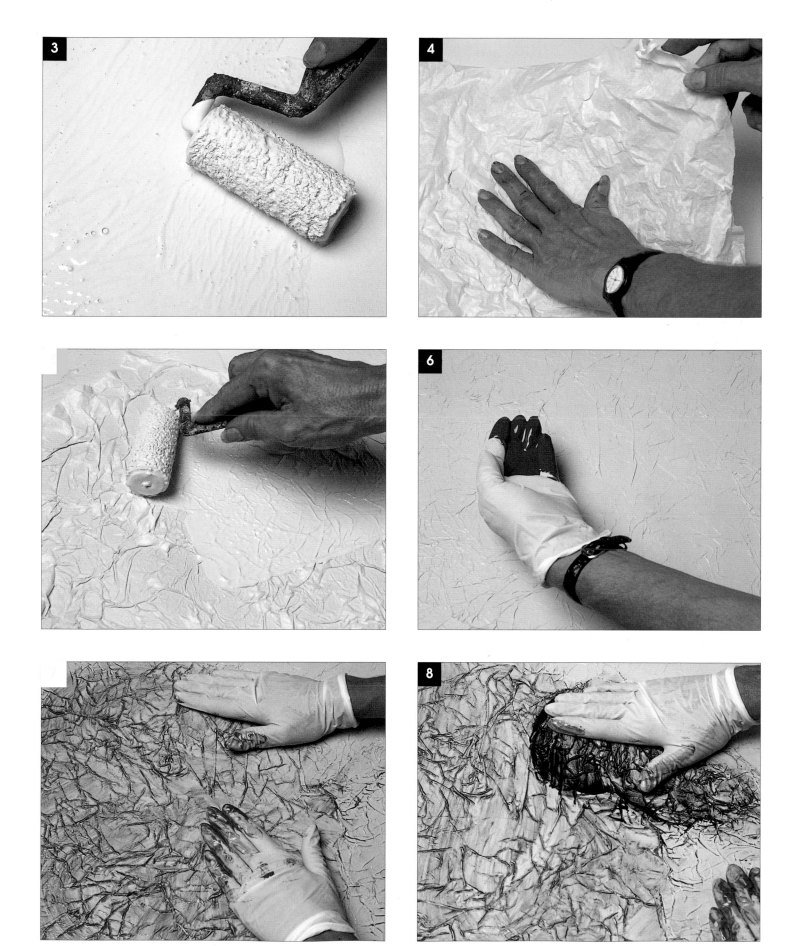

Beige Wall Treatment

Three earth-tone glaze colors are softly blended over tissue paper textured walls.
The effect is subtle and interesting.

Supplies

Basecoat – Putnam Ivory, a latex paint in eggshell sheen for painting walls

Glazes – Earth Brown, Green Umber, Van Dyke Brown, clear glazing medium + colorant to create the three colors of antiquing glaze

White tissue paper, enough to cover the square footage of the area you are texturing

4" paint roller and paint tray, for applying paint

Squeeze bottle, for holding glaze

Latex gloves, to protect your hands when applying the glaze

Painter's masking tape, to protect areas you don't wish to texture

Craft knife and metal straight edge, for removing tape

Instructions

See the "Procedure for Tissue Paper Texturing" in this section for details of this technique.

1. Tape off areas of the surface you are decorating that you aren't texturing or adjacent areas you wish to protect, such as trim.
2. Tear pieces of tissue paper into rough 12" or 18" squares. Crumple the torn pieces, then smooth them so they retain some wrinkles but are somewhat flat.
3. Working one wall section at a time, use a roller to apply a medium thick coat of Putnam Ivory paint.
4. While the paint is still wet, lay the wrinkled tissue pieces over the wet paint, using your hands to press the tissue to the wall.
5. Re-load the roller with paint and roll over the paper piece, working from the center of the paper-covered area outward to press out the air bubbles. Continue applying paint until the entire area is covered.
6. Repeat steps 3, 4 and 5 to cover all areas of the walls. Let dry completely (24 to 48 hours).
7. Put one color of glaze in a squeeze bottle, and put on latex gloves. Squeeze some glaze into your hand and use your gloved hands to rub the glaze on areas of the surface in all directions, allowing the glaze to settle in the wrinkles of the tissue, revealing the texture.
8. Add areas of the second glaze color. Lightly blend into edges of first color.
9. Apply the third glaze color to some areas and blend. Allow to dry completely.
10. Score edges and remove tape. ❏

Taupe Wainscoting

Tissue paper texturing provides a stunning texture for the lower walls in this kitchen. Striae glaze antiquing with the same paint and glaze colors was used on the wood trim for a monochromatic palette.

Décor designed by Euna Williams

Supplies

Basecoat – Lenox Tan latex paint in an eggshell sheen to paint lower walls and trim

Glaze – Mushroom, clear glazing medium + color to create the light brown antiquing glaze

White tissue paper, enough to cover the square footage of the area you are texturing

4" paint roller and paint tray, for applying paint

Squeeze bottle, for holding glaze

Latex gloves, to protect your hands when applying the glaze

Painter's masking tape, to protect areas you don't wish to texture

Craft knife and metal straight edge, for removing tape

Instructions

See the "Procedure for Tissue Paper Texturing" earlier in this section for details of this technique.

1. Mask off the trim.
2. Tear pieces of tissue paper into rough 12" or 18" squares. Crumple the torn pieces, then smooth them so they retain some wrinkles but are somewhat flat.
3. Working one wall section at a time, use a roller to apply a medium thick coat of Lenox Tan paint.
4. While the paint is still wet, lay the wrinkled tissue piece over the wet paint, using your hands to press the tissue to the wall.
5. Re-load the roller with paint and roll over the paper piece, working from the center of the tissue out-

ward to press out the air bubbles. Continue applying paint until the entire area is covered.

6. Repeat steps 3, 4 and 5 to cover all areas of the lower walls. Let dry completely (24 to 48 hours).
7. Put Mushroom glaze in a squeeze bottle, and put on latex gloves. Squeeze some glaze into one hand and use your gloved hands to rub the glaze on areas of the surface in all directions, allowing the glaze to settle in the wrinkles of the tissue, revealing the texture. Allow to dry completely.
8. Score and remove the tape. ❑

Black Walls

Black textured walls with old world bronze glaze highlighting are a dramatic contrast to lighter-color painted cabinets with striae glaze antiquing.

Décor designed by Euna Williams

Supplies

Basecoat – Universal Black a latex paint in an eggshell sheen to paint the walls

Glaze – Olde World Bronze a clear glazing medium + acrylic craft paint to create the antiquing glaze

White tissue paper, enough to cover the square footage of the area you are texturing

4" paint roller and paint tray, for applying paint

Squeeze bottle, for holding glaze

Latex gloves, to protect your hands when applying the glaze

Painter's masking tape, to protect areas you don't wish to texture

Craft knife and metal straight edge, for removing tape

Instructions

Follow the "Procedure for Tissue Paper Texturing" earlier in this section. ❏

Mirror Frame

Flat mirror or picture frames are excellent surfaces for tissue paper texturing since they allow you to create frames in the custom color of your choice.

Supplies

Base color – Avon Green, a latex paint in an eggshell sheen for painting the frame

Glaze – Green Umber, clear glazing medium + acrylic craft paint to create the antiquing glaze

White tissue paper, enough to cover the square footage of the area you are texturing

4" paint roller, for applying paint

Squeeze bottle, for holding glaze

Latex gloves, to protect your hands when applying the glaze

Painter's masking tape, to protect areas you don't wish to texture

Craft knife and metal straight edge, for removing tape

Sealer or varnish for final protective coat

Instructions

See the "Procedure for Tissue Paper Texturing" earlier in this section for details of this technique.

1. Tear pieces of tissue paper into rough 6" squares. Crumple the torn pieces, then smooth them so they retain some wrinkles but are somewhat flat.
2. Working one section at a time, use a roller to apply a medium thick coat of Avon Green paint.
3. While the paint is still wet, lay the wrinkled tissue piece over the wet paint, using your hands to press the tissue.
4. Re-load the roller with paint and roll over the paper piece, working from the center of the paper-covered area outward to press out the air bubbles. Continue applying paint and tissue until the entire area is covered.
5. Repeat steps 2, 3 and 4 to cover the frame. Let dry completely (24 to 48 hours).
6. Put Green Umber glaze in a squeeze bottle, and put on latex gloves. Squeeze some glaze into one hand and use your gloved hands to rub the glaze on the frame in all directions, allowing the glaze to settle in the wrinkles of the tissue. Allow to dry completely.
7. Apply sealer or varnish. ❑

130

Turquoise Candle Holders

You can also use tissue paper texturing to cover tabletop accessories.
To test your combination of paint and glaze, be sure to make
a sample board.

Supplies

Base color – Poolside Blue, a latex paint in an eggshell sheen for painting the candle sticks

Glaze – Leather Brown, clear glazing medium + colorant to create the antiquing glaze

White tissue paper, enough to cover the square footage of the area you are texturing

4" paint roller, for applying paint

Squeeze bottle, for holding glaze

Latex gloves, to protect your hands when applying the glaze

Painter's masking tape, to protect areas you don't wish to texture

Craft knife and metal straight edge, for removing tape

Sealer or varnish for final protective coat

Instructions

See the "Procedure for Tissue Paper Texturing" earlier in this section for details of this technique.

1. Tear pieces of tissue paper into rough 6" squares. Crumple the torn pieces, then smooth them so they retain some wrinkles but are somewhat flat.
2. Working one section of the surface at a time, use a roller to apply a medium thick coat of Poolside Blue paint.
3. While the paint is still wet, lay the wrinkled tissue piece over the wet paint, using your hands to press the tissue.
4. Re-load the roller with paint and roll over the paper piece, working from the center of the paper-covered area outward to press out the air bubbles. Continue applying

one piece at a time until the entire area is covered.
5. Repeat steps 2, 3 and 4 to cover the candle holders. Let dry completely (24 to 48 hours).
6. Put Leather Brown glaze in a squeeze bottle, and put on latex gloves. Squeeze some glaze into one hand and use your gloved hands to rub the glaze on the candle holders in all directions, allowing the glaze to settle in the wrinkles of the tissue. Allow to dry completely.
7. Apply sealer or varnish. ❑

Colorways

Colorway 1
Base color – Chili Pepper
Glaze – Espresso

Colorway 2
Base color – Chamois
Glaze – Raw Umber

Colorways

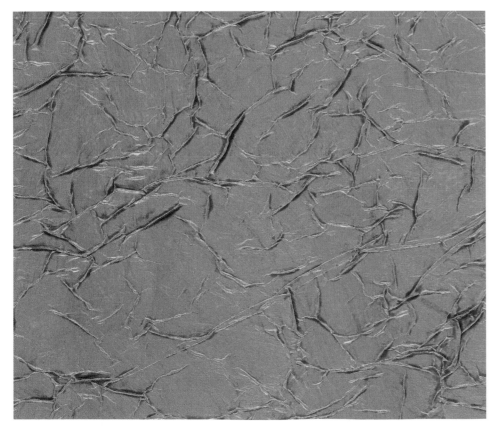

Colorway 3
Base color – Log Cabin
Glaze – Bittersweet Chocolate

Colorway 4
Base color – Woody Yellow
Glaze – Asphaltum

Colorway 5
Base color – Gold
Glaze – Golden Brown

Faux Metallic Leafing

Gilding and schaibin are techniques that take years to master. Real metal leafing is difficult to work with and expensive. That is why authentic leaf is usually seen on small items such as picture frames. Many products have emerged to simulate this exquisite process. The easiest and most cost effective of these is with the use of paint as you will discover in this chapter.

Schaibin. (or broken leaf) is a contemporary method of applying "broken" pieces or flakes of metal leaf to a surface, achieving actual metallic finishes. The finish is further enhanced by applying patinas or glazes, or by chemically tarnishing the metal surface. A similar look can be achieved with paint and glaze. This technique is called "faux broken leaf." With this technique, small random areas of the base coat still show through. These open areas are called "holidays."

The technique is ideal for enhancing small or intricately carved surfaces such as moldings, areas of a mantle or carved areas of furniture.

Furniture and other home decor accessories take on a dramatic, elegant look when you add faux broken leafing to accent raised or carved areas.

Gilding also uses real metal leaf. The authentic metal leaf is usually in 3" x 3" squares or 4" x 4" squares. The squares of thin metal leafing are applied to a surface one square at a time. When the leafing is complete, the squares are evident (and desired). The "Gold Metallic Squares" technique presented is done with paint, glaze, and tape.

This section explores these two techniques – broken leaf in selected areas and gold leafing applied in squares – that use metallic acrylic paint to mimic classic metal leafing techniques.

FAUX BROKEN LEAF
Basic Supplies

Paints

Latex paint – Dark color such as black, deep brown, or red, for basecoating to object

Metallic acrylic craft paint or other metallic paint, for the faux gold leafing

Glaze

Clear glazing medium, to mix with a color to create the glaze, and to also mix with gold paint

Colorants, paints or colored glazes in a dark color, for tinting the glazing medium

Tools & Other Supplies

Stencil brush, for applying paint

Chip brush, for applying glaze

Blue painter's masking tape, for masking off the leafing areas

Cheesecloth, for blotting the glaze

Spray bottle with water, to dampen the cheesecloth

Palette or disposable foam plates, to hold the metallic paint and glaze

Pictured left to right: Two stencil brushes, two chip brushes, cheesecloth, blue painter's tape, gold metallic acrylic paint

Procedure for Faux Broken Leafing

Basecoat the Piece

1. Basecoat the entire piece of furniture or other item with a dark color (black, deep brown, or red) of eggshell or satin latex paint. Allow to dry.

Mask with Tape

2. Mask off the area you are going to decorate with metallic to protect surrounding area. **(photo 1)**

Load the Brush

3. Add a little glazing medium to the metallic paint. Load a stencil brush by dipping it in the paint mixture. **(photo 2)**

Paint

4. Pounce the loaded brush on the area you have prepared, allowing some of the basecoat to show through. **(photo 3)**

5. Continue pouncing until you have completely treated the entire area, leaving some open areas or "holidays." Re-load your brush as needed. **(photo 4)** Let dry.
6. Remove the tape.

Glaze

7. To tone down the metallic color and add an antiqued look, brush a brown-tone glaze over the entire area, using a chip brush. Also brush some glaze on the surrounding area for blending. **(photo 5)**
8. While the glaze is still wet, spray water on a piece of folded cheesecloth (or a folded soft cloth) to dampen it. **(photo 6)**
9. Use a tapping motion to blot the glaze and soften the look in the gold-painted area with the damp cheesecloth. **(photo 7)**

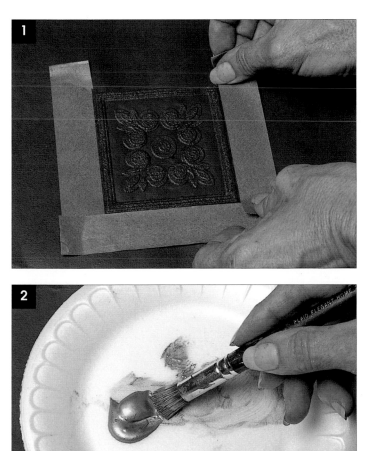

Procedure for Faux Broken Leafing Continued

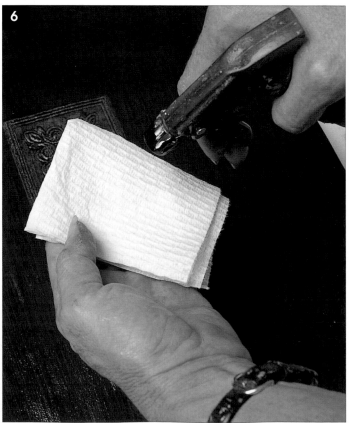

Gold Metallic Squares

This technique mimics the look of classic gilding applied in 3" x 3" or 4" x 4" squares. It is most effective on flat surfaces such as small sections of walls, room dividers, trays, and picture frames.
The dimension is created by a negative paint technique that uses plastic wrap to manipulate the paint.

Basic Supplies

Paints
Latex paint – Dark brown, dark red, or red brown, for the background

Gold metallic acrylic craft paint, for "leafing"

Glaze
Clear glazing medium, to mix with colorant to create the antiquing glaze, and to also mix with gold paint

Colorants (paints or colored glazes) in a dark color, for tinting the glazing medium

Tools & Other Supplies
Plastic wrap, for creating texture

1/8" wide masking tape, for masking off lines

1" sponge paint roller, for applying the gold paint

Cheesecloth, for applying antiquing glaze

Level, for measuring

Ruler, for measuring

Pencil, for marking

Paint brushes or paint roller and tray, for base painting

Palette or disposable foam plate, to hold the paint

Spray bottle with water, for dampening cheesecloth

Pictured clockwise from top: Cheesecloth, 1/8" wide tape, 1" sponge roller, plastic wrap

Procedure for Gold Metallic Squares

Achieve the look of authentic guilding using paint.

Prepare

1. Prepare the surface for painting, following the guidelines for cleaning, repairing, and priming in the section on "Surface Preparation."
2. Use drop cloths to protect the floor and adjacent surfaces.

Base Paint

3. Base paint the entire area to be finished with gold squares, using a dark brown, dark red, or black acrylic paint. Let dry completely.

Apply Tape

4. Measure and divide area into 3" x 3" squares. Use a straight edge and pencil to mark the lines. Place 1/8" wide tape on the lines creating a grid pattern. **(photo 1)** Burnish the tape lines with a spatula or credit card.

Paint

5. Mix a little glaze medium into the gold metallic paint, or use a gold pre-mixed glaze.
6. Pour some metallic gold glaze mixture on a palette or a disposable plate. Load the sponge roller with paint. **(photo 2)** Paint four of the squares with a heavy coat of gold paint glaze mixture, using the roller. Work one section at a time (4 squares) so you will have time to manipulate the paint before it dries. **(photo 3)**

Create Texture

7. Lay a piece of plastic wrap over the painted area. **(photo 4)** Press the wrap firmly to the surface, encouraging wrinkles **(photo 5)**.
8. Lift off the plastic wrap to reveal the texture. **(photo 6)** Discard the plastic wrap.
9. Repeat the steps until you have painted and textured the entire surface.

Remove Tape

10. As soon as you have finished painting and texturing the entire space, pull off the tape. **(photo 7)** The paint does not need to be dry; in fact, it is easier to remove the tape without harming the finish if the paint is still wet. Let paint dry completely, for at least 24 hours.

Apply Glaze

11. Spray water on a piece of cheesecloth to dampen. Dip the dampened cheesecloth in glaze. Rub brown glaze over the entire area, in a circular motion. This simulates normal tarnishing. **(photo 8)**
12. For a shiny finish, apply a satin sheen topcoat.

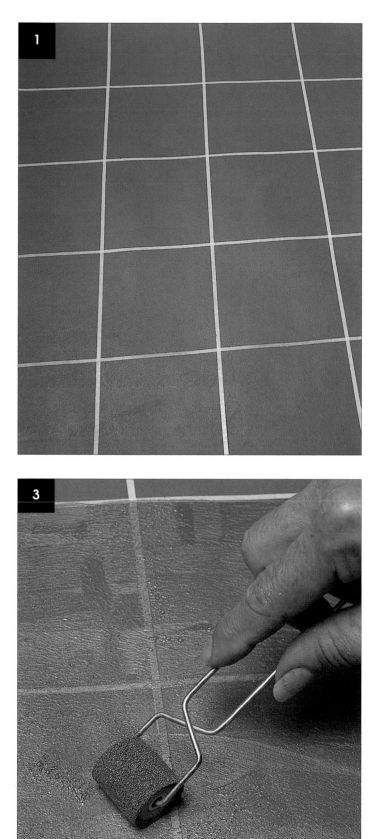

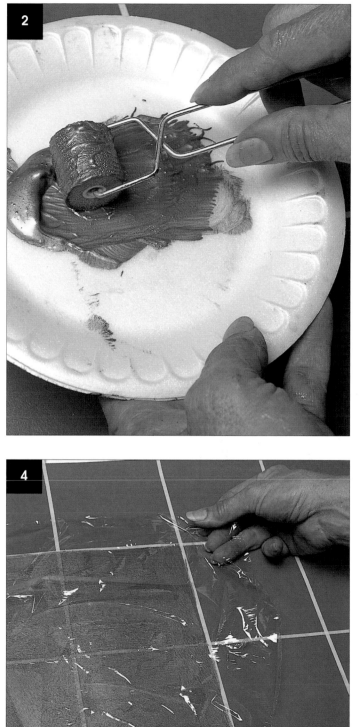

Continued on page 144

Gold Metal Square, Continued

Highlighting

Highlighting adds a look of formal elegance to surfaces, enhancing raised details and adding interest and dimension to embellishments that might otherwise go unnoticed, such as the carved areas of furniture pieces and mantles. Use this technique when you want to highlight a feature but not create the look of an applied embellishment.

To achieve this effect on unadorned surfaces, add carved wood, resin, or cast plaster embellishments before base painting, then add painted highlights. Since metallic highlights show up best on dark colors, choose black or another very dark color as a base. A brown-tone glaze, applied over the highlighting, tones down the harshness of the metallic paint. More subtle applications will give the appearance of a "rub through" without the need to sand.

Low Lighting goes hand in hand with highlighting. Low lighting helps to enhance recessed details on a surface, allowing the beauty of a design to stand out. This is achieved by glazing the carved or detailed area and allowing the glaze to settle in the low areas of the design. This is done after the piece is "highlighted." Low lighting can also be done without the highlighting step. It will give a more subtle look but still enhance the dimensional details.

Basic Supplies

Paints
Latex paint – a dark color, for base painting

Metallic acrylic craft paint – Gold, bronze, copper, or silver, for highlighting

Glaze
Clear glazing medium, for the glaze

Colorant (paints or colored glazes) such as Raw Umber, for tinting the glazing medium

Tools & Other Supplies
Foam brush, for applying highlights

Chip brush or other short-bristle brush, for applying glaze

Cheesecloth, for wiping away excess glaze

Spray bottle with water, for dampening cheesecloth

Palette or disposable foam plate, to use as a palette

Wet rag, for wiping off any mistakes

Paint brushes or paint rollers and tray, for base painting

Pictured left to right: two chip brushes, sponge brush, cheesecloth, acrylic craft paint, disposable plate

Continued on page 146

Procedure Instructions

Base Paint

1. Paint the furniture piece or mantle the color of your choice and allow to dry.

Load the Foam Brush

2. Squeeze some metallic paint on a disposable plate or palette. Load the flat angled edge of a foam brush with the paint metallic color. (here, I'm using bronze paint.) Dip and pull the brush from the puddle. **(photo 1)** Swirl the brush next to the puddle to make sure the paint is evenly distributed.

Highlight

3. Holding the brush like a pencil, lightly drag it over the raised areas, allowing the brush to touch only the tops of the raised places. Use a light, even pressure, and keep a wet rag at hand at all times for wiping off mistakes. **(photo 2)** Let dry.

Lowlight

This glazing step is called low lighting. It can be done after highlighting or done on its own.

4. Using a short bristle brush such as a chip brush, apply glaze (here, raw umber) over the entire piece, using a scrubbing, swirling motion so the glaze settles in the crevices. **(photo 3)**

5. While glaze is still wet, use a spray bottle to dampen a folded piece of cheesecloth. Wipe excess glaze from the piece, using the dampened cheesecloth, leaving the glaze in the crevices for a soft, dimensional look. **(photo 4)**

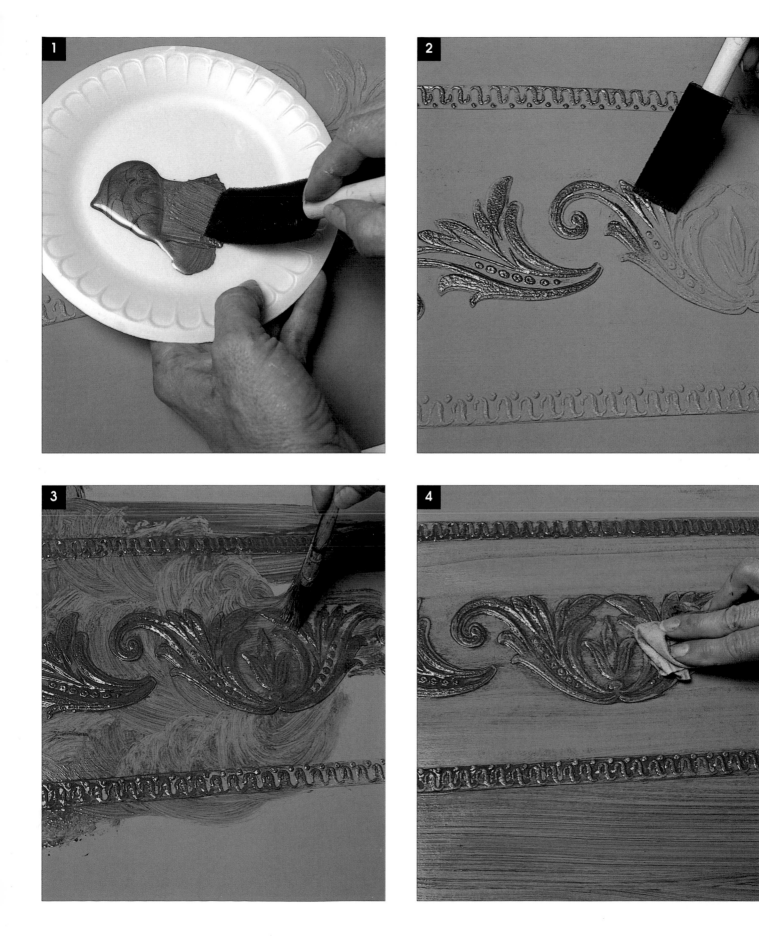

Black & Gold Mantle

Gold highlights ensure this mantle is the focal point of the room. Black and gold is
a classic combination.

Supplies

Basecoat – Bittersweet Chocolate, a latex paint in an eggshell sheen for painting the mantle

Acrylic craft paint – Metallic Gold for highlighting

Glaze – Black, clear glazing medium + colorant to create antiquing glaze

Foam brush, for applying highlights

Chip brush or other short-bristle brush, for applying antiquing

Cheesecloth, for wiping away excess glaze

Spray bottle with water, for dampening cheesecloth

Palette or disposable plate, to use as a palette

Wet rag, for wiping off any mistakes

Paint brushes or rollers, for base painting

Instructions

1. Paint the mantle with Bittersweet Chocolate. Allow to dry.
2. Squeeze some Gold paint on a disposable plate or palette. Load the flat angled edge of a foam brush.
3. Holding the brush like a pencil, lightly drag it over the raised areas, allowing the brush to touch only the tops of the raised places.
4. Using the photo as a guide, add some highlighting to the edges of the mantle. Let dry.
5. Using a short bristle brush such as a chip brush, apply Black glaze over the entire piece, allowing the glaze to settle in the low areas.
6. While glaze is still wet, use a damp piece of cheesecloth to wipe excess glaze from the piece. Leave the glaze in the crevices for a soft, antique look. ❏

Brown Mantle with Carved Wood Highlights

This mantle was highlighted after a stippled finish was applied.

Supplies

Basecoat – Universal Black a latex paint in eggshell sheen to paint mantel

Acrylic craft paint – Olde World Bronze for highlighting

Glaze – Espresso, clear glazing medium + colorant to create the antiquing glaze

Foam brush, for applying highlights

Chip brush or other short-bristle brush, for applying antiquing

Cheesecloth, for wiping away excess glaze

Spray bottle with water, for dampening cheesecloth

Palette or disposable plate, to use as a palette

Wet rag, for wiping off any mistakes

Paint brushes or rollers, for base painting

Instructions

1. Paint the mantle with Universal Black. Allow to dry.
2. Following the Procedure Instructions in the section on Stippling, use Burnt Umber glaze to apply a stippled finish. Let dry.
3. Squeeze some Olde World Bronze paint on a disposable plate or palette. Load the flat angled edge of a foam brush.
4. Holding the brush like a pencil, lightly drag it over the raised areas, allowing the brush to touch only the tops of the raised places. Let dry.
5. Using a short bristle brush such as a chip brush, apply Espresso glaze over the highlighted areas, allowing the glaze to settle in the crevices. (This is low lighting.)
6. While glaze is still wet, lightly blot areas where glaze is too heavy. Let dry. ❑

Closeup of mantle

Before

Lamps

Lamps are good candidates for metallic highlighting.
These highlighted lamps lend an elegant touch on a demi-lune table with faux broken leafing. Multiple procedures have been used to enhance the intricate dimensions of the lamps. The stems were crackled, while the details on the bases were highlighted with gold. A rich brown glaze was used to lowlight and soften the recessed areas.

GALLERY

Here are photos of some wonderful finishes that are a bit more advanced than the procedures in this book.
A custom finisher could create these looks.

These bathroom cabinets were given an "old iron" look.

Metallic Walls

This look was achieved using a technique of layered wax with embedded metallics.

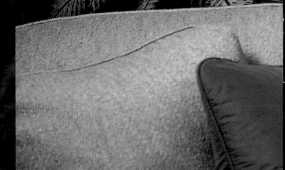

Metric Conversion Chart

Inches to Millimeters and Centimeters

Inches	MM	CM	Inches	MM	CM
1/8	3	.3	2	51	5.1
1/4	6	.6	3	76	7.6
3/8	10	1.0	4	102	10.2
1/2	13	1.3	5	127	12.7
5/8	16	1.6	6	152	15.2
3/4	19	1.9	7	178	17.8
7/8	22	2.2	8	203	20.3
1	25	2.5	9	229	22.9
1-1/4	32	3.2	10	254	25.4
1-1/2	38	3.8	11	279	27.9
1-3/4	44	4.4	12	305	30.5

Yards to Meters

Yards	Meters	Yards	Meters
1/8	.11	3	2.74
1/4	.23	4	3.66
3/8	.34	5	4.57
1/2	.46	6	5.49
5/8	.57	7	6.40
3/4	.69	8	7.32
7/8	.80	9	8.23
1	.91	10	9.14
2	1.83		

Index

Continued on next page

Index